TESTIMONIALS

"Sharing her experience has helped me and others take a deep look at our lives and our relationships. I know all who can experience the *marrsing* journey will find this very impactful to their lives and the lives of the partners they choose. I am deeply honored to be a part of Angella's life and most importantly, the *marrsing* journey. I know this is only the beginning."

— **Jennifer James**, MBA, MPFP, MST,
Consulting CFO, Acacia Business

"I met Angella on a beach in Jamaica. The first time we saw each other, we spontaneously started to talk. It was beautiful on the beach, the weather was perfect, and we exchanged in such an easy way like we had known each other for a long time. The power of communication was real and we talked for hours. I even saw in Angella a 'joie de vivre' rare with Anglophones. There was a kindness and I wanted to know more about the person sitting there on the beach. Her openness to converse with me, a Canadian, and her positive view made this meeting a fun morning. I could feel her love for life and her acknowledgement to others around her. Her appreciation of life makes us want to continue talking, exchanging. We covered many subjects in such a positive manner; it was delightful, and I sincerely hope that her readers will appreciate the message in her book. Conscientiousness of others is definitely a plus in our world."

— **Marielle Poirier**, French Canadian Retired Teacher

"*The Power of Marrsing* gives us more than food for thought for anyone who wants to create a loving, honest, authentic relationship. By promoting self-awareness as an integral part of any relationship, Angella Watkis Francis is inviting us to live intentionally, to love consciously, and to share generously. From this perspective, it is not about love itself, but how each one of us uses love as a driving force to create a mutually beneficial, respectful, and committed relationship. I loved the comparison of an intimate relationship with financial wealth, reminding us that nothing grows without commitment and investment. Through Angella's personal experience, both raw and funny, important messages are shared. It is so important to be reminded that each one of us is the value we bring to any relationship and we create the reality of our lives."

— **Angela Silva Mendes**, Author of *Getting There By Being Here*, Founder of Upanji Life Coaching, Connecticut, USA

"You may not know the term *marrsing*, but you can trust that Angella Francis will reveal this new way of looking deep within yourself for the answers you seek in your primary relationship. Angella has pulled together some of the most prolific insights from philosophers and religious text in order to support you in creating the kind of relationship you desire. Insightful, easy to understand, and immediately actionable. A fast and effective read."

— **Bill Carmody**, Bestselling Author of *The Three Rules of Marriage*

"Angella and I met twenty-five years ago through her cousin, my husband of nineteen years now. Her words are spoken from the heart, a heart which is always open to every human being who desires to know her. Angie's book can help each and every one of us reflect and grow as individuals but also in our relationships with one another. Nous t'aimons tous très fort, Angie! (We all love you very much, Angie!)"

— **Christelle Millet-Robinson**, Registered Nurse, New Jersey, USA

"I never thought of examining or working on my individual self before reading this book or loving me before being ready to give and receive love, but I suppose it makes sense. When you know who you are and are happy with yourself, then you will be able to love and communicate effectively with a partner. This book has truly helped me to examine my relationship with my husband of twenty-one years. I am totally invested and committed in my relationship, love has flourished, and there have been many ups and downs, mainly due to communication issues—so I am looking forward to applying the *marrsing* principles to myself first and then to the relationship with my husband. This is a great read with powerful points for everyone, married or single."

— **Karen Hunter**, Teacher, London, England

"Dearest Angella—What a very special person you are. Meeting you for the first time and talking with you felt like I have known you for years. Now, celebrating with you on your up and coming book, thank you for sharing your experience, this book will heal, inspire, encourage, and restore as readers discover their inner strength and self worth. I thank God for birthing this book within you and He will faithfully take you to completion and beyond."

— **Angela Miller**, England, UK

"Angella, I so appreciate you. You are a beautiful woman with phenomenal strength. Your laughter is like no other, your kindness, generosity, and vivacious ways are enchanting. I thank you for your open honesty and for allowing us to share your vulnerability. It's a privilege to know such a virtuous woman. *Marrsing* is captivating and inspiring, it's healing and soul searching. One in which physicality and spirituality are explored and inner strength is found. By God's grace, he will carry you through this journey. Don't cry because it's over, smile because it happened! May the Lord continue to inspire and bless you."

— Much love from **Claudette Miller**, England

"Angella, you are a beautiful soul. We have shared so many wonderful memories. Thank you so much for just being you, you're a true gift to those who are privileged to know you. My gratitude to you for sharing this inspirational book on your own experiences. You have shown strength and tenacity. This holistic approach to relationships has enlightened and inspired me.

It's engaging, fascinating, motivating, and informative. I thank God that He has inspired you to explore the concept of *marrsing* and for a realistic approach in bringing this powerful book to us, to evaluate the significance of our well-being. May the words from your mouth and the meditation of your heart impact the mind, heart, and soul of the readers."

— **Pamela Miller**, Birmingham, England

The Power of
MARRSING

Tapping into Our Individual Consciousness

The Power of
MARRSING

Tapping into Our Individual Consciousness

Understanding How the Purpose, Power,
and Passion within the **Individual Self**
Influences and Defines Our **Commitment**
in Relationships and Marriages

Angella Watkis Francis

PYP

PUBLISH
YOUR
PURPOSE
PRESS

For permission requests, write to the publisher, addressed "Attention: Permissions Coordinator," at the address below.

Publish Your Purpose Press
141 Weston Street, #155
Hartford, CT, 06141

The opinions expressed by the Author are not necessarily those held by Publish Your Purpose Press.

Ordering Information: Quantity sales and special discounts are available on quantity purchases by corporations, associations, and others. For details, contact the publisher at orders@publishyourpurposepress.com.

Edited by: Tamera Bryant, Nancy Graham-Tillman, and Chloë Siennah
Cover design by: Cornelia Murariu
Typeset by: Medlar Publishing Solutions Pvt Ltd., India

Printed in the United States of America.
ISBN: 978-1-951591-48-9 (paperback)
ISBN: 978-1-951591-49-6 (ebook)

Library of Congress Control Number: 2021919682

First edition, December 2021.

The information contained within this book is strictly for informational purposes. The material may include information, products, or services by third parties. As such, the Author and Publisher do not assume responsibility or liability for any third-party material or opinions. The publisher is not responsible for websites (or their content) that are not owned by the publisher. Readers are advised to do their own due diligence when it comes to making decisions.

The mission of Publish Your Purpose Press is to discover and publish authors who are striving to make a difference in the world. We give underrepresented voices power and a stage to share their stories, speak their truth, and impact their communities. Do you have a book idea you would like us to consider publishing? Please visit PublishYourPurposePress.com for more information.

DEDICATION

*I dedicate this book to
my mother Joyce, my children Jamahl, Rashaun, Kevaun, and Neil,
my true, heart-touching friends, my relatives through both blood and love,
and to every person who believes in their individual power to love
and remain committed to another human being despite the challenges.*

*I wrote this book to
share, educate, inspire, and to encourage positivity
in ourselves and our relationships.*

CONTENTS

TO MY READERS

This is my GIFT to you and a legacy to the world. Read it with an expectation to be transformed in yourself and your important relationships. I hope it will expand your mind towards next level awareness.

This book was written as a compilation of the knowledge, understanding, and wisdom that I am sharing on the Marrsing Concept. Therefore, you may choose to read it sequentially chapter by chapter or choose specific chapters that are inviting to you. I hope you will enjoy this gift. Every word is being sent with positive Energy!

— **Angella Watkis Francis,**
The Power of Marrsing

FOREWORD

I am so proud to recognize Angella Watkis-Francis as my best friend for life. Our friendship of forty-two years has grown from accompanying each other for outdoor nighttime showers and discussing everything from birth control to diaper choices. We pinky swore at eleven years old to be maids of honor in each other's weddings and godparents to our children. We have reveled in each other's children's successes and built them back up after their disappointments. We have enjoyed the success of our relationships and comforted each other when they've failed. Our yearly birthday travels of over thirty years started out in Jamaica, evolving to the likes of Switzerland, Japan, Italy, and Iceland.

This was all possible due to this incredible woman, Angella Watkis-Francis. She is so generous, it is contagious. I have attended three weddings where I can attest to her generosity—she brought more guests than seats allowed, but Angella's love for her friends and family would not allow her to leave anyone out, even if they had to sit on the floor.

That smile of hers lights up every room she enters. Her persona draws old friends near and creates new friends wherever she goes. Her charisma allows her to lead, listen, and enhance any conversation. Even during her time of personal disappointment, Angella found time to lift the spirit of her friends and family.

Her spunk is what continues to lift her forward. I am so proud to see Angella complete her *marrsing* book. This therapeutic narration has profoundly changed Angella's life. Her sharing of her experience has helped me and others take a deep look at our lives and our relationships with our family. I know all who can experience the *marrsing* journey will find this very impactful in their lives and the lives of the partners they choose.

I am deeply honored to be a part of Angella's life and most importantly, the *marrsing* journey. I know this is only the beginning of a new path she is creating for others to follow.

— **Jennifer James**, MBA, MPFP, MST,
Consulting CFO, Acacia Business

INTRODUCTION

Marrsing = Marr (commitment/marriage) sing (individual self)
Marrsing: The energy created from being conscious versions of
our individual *self* and being a partner/spouse in a committed
relationship or marriage.

I created the term *marrsing* from the word *married* for the commitments
we make as partners and *single* as in the individual *self* (rather than as a
relationship status). *Marrsing* is an inclusive concept of our energy and consciousness surrounding intimate relationships and marriages. If we are truly
open to intentional living, conscious loving, and compassionate and generous
sharing when committing to our partners, it leads us on a path of questioning,
acknowledging, and understanding our self and our relationship patterns.

I use the terms *commitment, relationship, marriage,* and *partnership* both
together and interchangeably throughout this book to represent the many
aspects of a committed, intimate, interpersonal connection. I respect each
couple's decision to define their relationship with whomever they choose to
love. I respect how couples choose to validate their connection, whether it
is by having a wedding ceremony, signing legal documents, adhering to cultural norms, cohabitating, or simply committing to each other symbolically.

Our relationships are designed by us—the people in them. Therefore, only we as the individuals who establish relationships have the power to truly create, define, and terminate them.

The power of *marrsing* acts as a guide for becoming more conscious versions of ourselves and helps us transform our thoughts and actions toward creating harmonious relationships and marriages.

THE VALIDATION OF MARRSING

Throughout the years, many best-selling authors, philosophers, experienced professionals, and talented individuals have written about the intricacies of relationships. They have researched, preached, and counseled about the complexities of the "single individual self" and two human beings trying to exist as one unit through the many stages of life, love, and maturity. I have been enriched by their pioneering contributions, expertise, knowledge, and wisdom about the inner workings of our minds, spirits, and bodies. Over the past 100 years, they have produced a myriad of resources for us to avail ourselves to. I appreciate the contributions their work has made to my knowledge and wisdom, and in understanding the powers within the "single self" that each of us brings into our relationships and marriages as an energy we can now recognize as *marrsing*.

CHAPTER 1

MARRSING COMMUNICATIONS

*Good communication will often make the difference between
success and failure. Good communication requires understanding
and empathy. Seek to relate with people on their terms.
The relationships you forge will be rewarding, indeed.*

— Ralph Marston

*Man is made or unmade by himself. In the armory of thought,
he forges the weapons by which he destroys himself. He also fashions
the tools with which he builds for himself heavenly mansions
of joy and strength and peace.*

— James Allen

I remain passionately curious about the magical energy of love and commitment and their effects on the human psyche. As an energy and lifestyle concept, *marrsing* is beneficial for anyone seeking a more harmonious and synergistic relationship both within themselves and in marriage and fully committed relationships. I invite you to embrace your *marrsing* energy by acknowledging that there is always room for improvement within ourselves as an individual and in our relationships as a partner or spouse.

My purpose in writing this book is to benefit and contribute to the betterment of intimate partner relationships and marriages. The treasures of my marriage are worthy to be curated and shared. The knowledge, wisdom, and experiences are valuable. With this book, it is my hope to inspire and motivate partners and spouses to use the power of *marrsing* to enhance their own individual well-being and transform their relationships. I also hope to help them identify what is important in their marriages and relationships and show them how they can direct their thoughts and actions toward the true purpose they committed to achieving as partners. *Marrsing* helps remind us to contemplate our thoughts so we can check ourselves for energy blockages and emotional bleeds that can interfere with our authenticity and affect our vulnerability. It can help us boost our emotional strength and empower us to operate at a higher level of consciousness, despite the actions of the other partner.

Life rewards us with peace, harmony, and contentment when we experience love for ourselves and from those we trust, admire, and respect.

Craving attention from a committed person is inherent in our human nature whether it is parental, romantic, or compassionate love. The need to be nurtured, romanced, or empathized with is evident from the day we are born until the day we die. As babies, we cry constantly until someone holds us close to their heart, reassuring us that we are loved and cared for. As adults, we begin to yearn for a partner who is going to care about us, adore us, and satisfy our inherent need to feel wanted and loved. In our last days and hours of life, we want our loved ones to be with us as we transition. Our emotions are constantly seeking other emotional signals to connect with.

But how do we effectively communicate our emotions to each other throughout the span of our relationships and marriages? What patterns and signs should we be consciously aware of in our interactions that will convey the true meaning of each other's feelings? How do we decide when to switch our communication channels? When we are connecting with our partner, are we willing to reveal our true inner self and genuinely share that authentic self within our committed relationships and marriages? How do we lovingly, respectfully, and appreciatively navigate and embrace the competing thoughts of self and partner?

Relationships are about communicating and connecting. Everything—good and bad—that happens between partners and spouses is directly related to communication whether it is through the way we dress, walk, interact, or deliver our expressions. Communication signals can be weak with static confusion, noise meanness, and disrespectfulness. Or they can be strong with good vibrations, clarity, positive intentions, kindness, and respectfulness. Communication affects the health and harmony of our relationships. Transmitted in deception and dishonesty, communication will cause chaos and distrust in our interactions. True and sincere communication will invite great positive and harmonious energies into our spirit, environment, and home.

When the channels of communication are clear, strong, and accurately understood, relationships can be beautiful and peaceable. Can you imagine having the tools and a mutually arranged set of agreements that truthfully translate feelings and ideas into the same mental picture that allow both partners and spouses to understand and appreciate the value of communication? What about having a concept that conjures up the appropriate emotions and reactions in our minds as we listen with heartfelt consciousness? What would change if we began listening, not just to words, but also to the communicator's intention? These are questions I continue to explore in hopes of bridging the gaps in communication within intimate relationships and marriages.

Our modes and methods of communication are constantly evolving. At one time, texting and other advancements in technology were considered inappropriate for intimate communications. Now, technology is a dominant player in our relationships. Depending on how we feel, think, and converse, and based on how we send and receive them, our messages will change in meaning, timing, and perception.

Our different perceptions and influences are hard at work both consciously and subconsciously in our communication fields. As human beings, we have a myriad of emotions that quickly jump in and hijack our transmission signals and distort our interactions when we communicate. These emotions hold our thoughts hostage until we can consciously negotiate with our current state of mind to find a rational solution and an appropriate reaction to what we are experiencing. The solutions are never a "one-size-fits-all" bundle of do's and don'ts. What works well in one marriage or relationship is not guaranteed to work in another.

The experiences that color our life are intricately woven into the unique, single individual we bring into our relationships and marriages. The way we communicate is directly related to our inner thoughts and feelings and to the person we have evolved into as a partner or spouse in our committed relationship.

We are only capable of offering love, care, and compassion if we have it inside us. What is inside us gets poured into our relationships through thoughts, feelings, and actions. Within our subconscious intentions and convictions, we have the innate power to create the relationships and marriages we desire. Before we can truly care for another person, though, we have to understand our own innate, authentic self. We must genuinely and honestly accept ourselves as the uniquely designed single individuals we are, including all our flaws and idiosyncrasies.

American author Napoleon Hill, a leading writer in the modern thought movement in accomplishing personal goals and author of the 1937 popular self-help book *Think and Grow Rich*, tells us, "The human mind responds to stimuli through which it may be 'keyed up' to high rates of vibration, known as enthusiasm, creative imagination, intense desire, etc. The stimuli to which the mind responds most freely [the top three] are:

1. The desire for sex expression,
2. Love, **and**
3. A burning desire for fame, power, financial gain, money."[1]

These are the three strongest forms of stimulation that have the intensity to distort other vibrational signals and entice us to disregard our responsibilities and other demands of our life, partner, and family. This means our minds are: more attuned for sexual pleasure, the emotions and expressions of love, and the status and possessions that will give us more opportunity for both sex and love. Most of us yearn to experience love and can fall (in love) with no controllable guidance for the person we believe is *the one*. We believe that this is the partner who is going to give us what we lack or what we are yearning for in the form of power (status), fame (significance), or material riches (money). We may marry and pledge to love and stay with each other 'til death do us part, intentionally hoping for the fairytale ending of living our happily ever after. However, deep within our souls, our inner inhibitions, suppressed contradictions, and addictions wrestle with our contradicting thoughts, suppressed desires, and inherent personalities.

Relationships are connections and movements of energy in the universe. Our energies are created from past experiences, inherent tendencies, and self-pleasing characteristics that each of us brings into our relationships. They eventually manifest into countless constructive or destructive emotional energies based on how we translate and navigate the accompanying thoughts and emotions. If we do not manage the destructive ones and prevent them from controlling us, they will wreak havoc on our relationships, marriages, and homes.

Happiness in life depends on the quality of our thoughts. Roman philosopher of stoicism Marcus Aurelius, who was recognized as one of the Five Good Emperors, his thoughts on the moral tenets of stoicism in *Meditations* has been interpreted to modern language as: "To understand the true quality of people, we must study into their minds and examine their pursuits and aversions."[2] He further says, "We must be mindful and intentional that we do not entertain notions that are contradictory to our virtues and reasonable to our nature."[3] A frequently quoted modern day statement credited to a translation of *Meditations* is, "The true worth of a man is measured by the objects he pursues." So, if we find ourselves spending time and energy on things and people who are not aligned with our aspirational future, then we should redirect that energy and time toward the purpose we want to achieve. In his book *Rich Dad Poor Dad*, American author Robert Kiyosaki says, "Too many people are focused too much on money and not their greatest wealth, which is their education. If people are prepared to be flexible, keep an open mind and learn, they will grow richer and richer through the changes."[4] Even though he said it in the context of financial education and wealth, it applies to the value of our relationships.

If we are not sincere and honest in how we communicate in our relationships, our lies will unravel when the truth surfaces. When we are building our committed, emotional connections, anything less than intentional honesty about our behaviors, actions, and aspirations will eventually cause our relationships to fail.

Dishonesty destroys the value of our committed relationships. When we indulge in secrecy, cover-ups, and half-truths, we end up deceiving, mistrusting, and misleading each other. When deception and dishonesty entice desirous sexual actions outside of committed relationships, it bankrupts the emotional investments of the relationship. This can result in tectonic emotional rifts of burning tensions and raw emotions that can mimic a volcanic eruption.

Whatever we are passionately striving for is defined as our purpose. We align our purpose with the people and circumstances we can influence and change toward what we want to accomplish. As we mature and gain wisdom about being conscious partners in our committed relationships and marriages, we begin to recognize that our thoughts and actions matter not just to us but to the other person as well. This awareness invokes in ourselves a sense of responsibility and a desire to understand that there is always room for improvement in how we live, love, and share with our partner and spouse.

Marrsing empowers us to align our intentions with our purpose and become keepers of our commitments. It enhances our zest for life, cultivates energies of affection, and ignites spirits of generosity and empathy toward one another.

Learning to acknowledge our individual worth gives us the reassurance that no one can deplete us unless we internalize thoughts of depletion. We can learn to embrace our value with a sense of gratitude, even for the mundane abilities that we take for granted. Cultivating gratitude rewards us with abundance and contentment. Embracing a spirit of abundance fills us with innate value and empowerment, allowing us to live intentionally, love consciously, and share generously toward our purpose—regardless of the circumstances and environment we are operating in.

Our happiness comes from our inner world, which is created from our thoughts. Life is a true reflection of our life choices. The repetitive and contemplative thoughts inside us will manifest and create our desires in the outer world. What are your true desires for your relationship and marriage?

As we embrace the *marrsing* concept, our conscious awareness begins acknowledging the flow of universal energy from our singularity (our *self*) into our marriages and relationships. This empowering cognition will help us untangle the competing emotions that can hijack the communication field and interfere with our ability to align our actions with our commitment to each other.

Marrsing Thought

A higher level of consciousness elevates and expands our mental capacity to own our truths.

Angella Watkis Francis

PURPOSE—AN INTENTIONAL JOURNEY

*The God who gave you the grace to start will give
you the grace to finish.*

— Joel Osteen

*If we want our home and our surroundings happy,
we need to be happy first. We can transform everything
around us, if we transform ourselves.*

— James Allen

The journey we are on in life and in our relationships are all because of the choices we make. The options are not always going to be what we expect, but as long as we understand who we are authentically, and what our purpose is supposed to be, we'll be able to own our power and stand with our decisions, despite the outcome. Talk show host, author, and philanthropist Oprah Winfrey publishes a column entitled "What I Know for Sure" in the back of her monthly publication of *O Magazine*. This column has contributed to the development of my innate ability to sense individual energies and better understand our human capacity to add to or subtract from our worth and whether we choose to diminish or improve our individual self. One notable quote that was also included in the book with same title inspires me: "I know for sure: Your journey begins with a choice to get up, step out, and live fully."[1] For the tenth year anniversary of the magazine, I went to the event-filled weekend celebration in New York City and came away with a stronger conviction of how our experiences prepare us for the destiny ahead. I became even more resolute in my spirituality to keep trusting God to guide my choices.

LOVE INTUITION FROM 13 TO 31

LOVE is the strongest magnetic force in the universe.

— John Kehoe

In his lecture on the book *The Biology of Belief,* author and developmental biologist Bruce Lipton says, "Love is the greatest growth signal in the world. When we are experiencing joy and love, we are well. Love, life, and happiness all come from being loved and being well."[1] When I was thirteen years old, I met this tall, dark-skinned, nineteen-year-old guy at a Saturday night bingo party. I was sitting one seat in front of him while my mother sat three seats ahead of me. This mischievous guy and I had an immediate attraction to each other, and I flirted with him by playfully switching his bingo card with mine. After bingo was over, he told me he admired my lively spirit and wanted to see me again. These were the days before the prevalence of cell phones, so we had to make plans to meet in person. The following month, he asked me to stop by his house on my way home from school. Even though I was an inexperienced girl, I was aware of the workings of a teenage boy's mind, obsessively filled with thoughts of "getting" with a girl rather than being in a relationship. For the next several months, whenever I stopped by to see him, I was smart enough to stay outside his house and talk.

I became infatuated with his charm and impressed by his willingness to patiently continue courting me. After deep contemplation about the intentions of this older man who had stolen my heart, I began thinking about his worthiness to win the prize—*me*. I decided to test the compatibility of our universal energy with a predictive cross-out game, which is a simple exercise that uses two full names as a mathematical equation. Players cross out the letters in each name that are similar, then repeat "love, like, dislike" as they go through each of the remaining letters. If the feelings match it would be a go for the relationship. Fast forward almost forty years later, I now realize the resulting emotions from the game were indicative of the future state of our destination.

I played the game to see if he would be the one to take my teenage innocence. This small, intentional exercise of three simple deciding words became the foundation of creating a life path together. A journey that has led to 3.1 children, a thirty-one-year marriage, and almost forty years of learning and evolving from the experiences and wisdom of being in a committed relationship.

I am a lifelong learner. I believe there is always a lesson available to teach us how to grasp new concepts and grow our knowledge base. Throughout my experiences, I have become more consciously aware of being more intuitive and attentive to my personal energy levels, number patterns, and individual traits. Being observant of our own *self* and of others tells us so much more than the words we hear or the way things seem, a significant lesson that I retrospectively recognized. I became consciously aware of a few number patterns that have significance in my life.

Meeting my first husband at the tender age of thirteen was too young an age for a grown-up relationship to manifest and last. So, God's guidance created a migration departure that spanned three years, and then another three years long distance before we got married. I will share more of these significances that include the numbers *one* and *three* later in this book: age *13*, *31* cents, *3.1* children, and *31* years.

The universe opens and closes chapters of my life with the numbers one and three. It is one of God's ways of letting me know that if I keep faith, trust the process, and follow his guidance, it will work out alright. This has strengthened my confidence in understanding that this is the life God ordained for me. It is aligned with my "go to" Bible scripture in Proverbs 3:5–6: "Trust in the Lord with all thine heart. Lean not on your own understanding, in all thy ways acknowledge him, and he will direct your path." These words have guided, calmed, and reassured me through many decisions and challenges. As I reflect regularly on my personal, family, and marital journeys, I know for sure that God is always communicating with us. We miss the communication signals when we exist in disharmony, chaos, and negativity. It is important to carve out time and space (even if it is in the bathroom) to be quiet and "tune in" (not just hear) to our body, mind, and spirit. Being "in-tune" allows us to recognize meanings and acknowledge signals. Florence Scovel Shinn, writer of illustrative books and thought leader in positive affirmations of the mid-1900s, writes in her book *The Power of the Spoken Word*, "Intuition is a spiritual faculty and it does not explain, but simply points the way."[2] Our intuition is God's communication signal to us.

I am fundamentally inspired and guided by the doctrines in the Bible and our existence within the cosmic laws of the universe. Through the years, I developed a remarkable curiosity to analyze the inner workings of the individual *self* and the interconnectedness of human beings in relationships. Throughout our thirty-one years as partners, my husband and I have traveled each chapter of our life together gathering a wealth of wisdom that has sparked my awareness and cultivated my creative consciousness to be open for the next phase. All this knowledge, wisdom, and experience became the fundamental tenet of *marrsing*.

Every one of us, as a single individual in a marriage or relationship, infuses who we are and what we have within us into our relationships. We are responsible for half of the marriage and half of the energy circulating within the relationship. We hold the control mechanism for the thoughts, feelings, and behaviors that we communicate and tolerate within the union. If we insist on only satisfying our individual emotions, needs, and aspirations, then there is going to be disharmony and eventually dissolution of our relationships.

Our internal world subconsciously plays out in our external physical existence. Everything that goes on in our minds contributes to the way we live, love, and share our affection and possessions. Thread by thread, these experiences are sewn together as the fabric of our lives to create the outfits of the single *self*. In his book *The Book of Secrets*, Deepak Chopra, spiritual leader, Clinical Professor of Family Medicine and Public Health at the University of California, and best-selling author of over ninety books says, "The way you think, the way you behave, the way you eat, can influence your life for the next thirty to fifty years."[3]

American essayist and philosopher Ralph Waldo Emerson says, "We know that the ancestor of every action is a thought."[4] It's our individual thoughts that will determine if we choose to respect or disrespect, love or hate, and appreciate or mistreat our partners within the sphere of our relationships.

The thoughts, perceptions, and feelings that we bring into our relationships and marriages are products of ourselves. Through the days, months, and years, we will consistently question our emotions and reasons for being and staying together. When the basic foundational elements of our marital and committed relationship structures are not intentionally aligned to create a stable foundation, the platform will eventually collapse and cause the marriage and relationship structure to crumble. Therefore, to endure the tests of relationship storms, it is important to understand that we are all different and have varying expectations that require many discussions. We must define a goal—a definite purpose for our relationship—then align our intentions and actions with the goal we want to accomplish as partners together.

If our intentions do not align, we will fail in our communication with each other. When this happens, both partners are responsible for the miscommunication and should acknowledge and work toward improving the synergy. Human nature, however, does not give in to accepting fault or blame so easily. Unless we are engaged in regular dialogue and mutual understanding, there are going to be miscalculations that will negatively affect the relationship and marriage environment. We must exercise good management of the communication channels we are responsible for. Think about the person who is receiving our messages when we communicate. Each one of us needs to consider the delivery and reception of our expressions if we want to enhance and transform our relationships and marriages.

With *marrsing*, we can contemplate our intentions and decipher the feelings behind our thoughts, the words we use, and the behaviors we practice. In his book *The Power of Intention: Learning to Co-create Your World Your Way*, self-help author Wayne Dyer says, "Silent knowledge starts when you invite the power of intention to play an active part in your life. This is a personal choice that needn't be explained or defended. When you make this inner choice, silent knowledge will gradually become a part of your normal, everyday awareness. By banishing doubt and trusting your intuitive feelings, you clear a space for the power of intention to flow through."[5] Despite unacceptable behaviors from our partners, we still get to choose our own state of mind.

What is the reality we want to experience in our relationships? Are we in it only to benefit and satisfy the single person within? Is the union, which we exuberantly vowed to each other to uphold until the day we die, just a cloak of security for the buried childhood disappointments and traumatic experiences that happened in our lives?

Marrsing enriches and empowers us to create and attain the interpersonal relationships that transform our well-being and our lives. It starts with acknowledging our truest *self*, controlling our thoughts, understanding our relationship patterns, and developing a mutual relationship blueprint plan that will result in emotional harmony between partners. *Marrsing* encourages the expression of intentional truths about who we are, what we want, and how we want it. We get to discover how we can serve our partner and avoid regretful reactions and destructive responses.

It is prudent for us to allow the spirit and energy of God's will to anchor us in our relationships rather than be influenced by the ever-blowing winds of our reactionary will. This means choosing God's guiding words to direct our thoughts and paths and keeping positive, affirming words, quotes, and scriptures rooted in our hearts and minds. We must release things and people from our psyche who are not beneficial to our flow and who no longer contribute to our energy in a positive way. In his 2012 television broadcast resurrection sermon *Power for Living*, author and religious leader Bishop Dale Bronner quoted Benjamin Franklin when he cautioned, "Don't keep the unwanted guests around … unwanted guests and rotten fish start stinking after three days."[6] Negativity is like a bad stench. When we hold onto negative things, people, or emotions too long, they begin to stink. Harboring a spirit of negativity and keeping ongoing malice will contaminate and deplete us.

Experiencing *marrsing* sets our intentions toward our aspirations and goals in our committed relationships, immersing us in the conscious awareness of our authentic inner *self* to truly love someone and be committed through the spirit of love. It is a serendipitous path of exemplary experiences, psychological awareness, and intuitive God-force wisdom that creates a transformative journey that can then be embraced.

THE GIFT OF LOVE

Love is the center of Human life.

— The Dalai Lama

To become masters of Love,
we have to practice Love.

— Don Miguel Ruiz

Our life story is ours to create. As authors of our lives, we get to choose and direct the plot. Experiencing love for ourselves and from our partner in our relationship and marriage is truly a choice we make from our inner dialogue and our intentions. In his book *The Spontaneous Fulfillment of Desire, Harnessing the Infinite Power of Coincidence*, the spiritual philosopher Deepak Chopra says, "Positive inner dialogue helps move us in the right direction, foster synchronicity, and promotes spiritual development."[1] Recognizing God's power within us at an early age is a gift in life.

At thirteen years old, anticipating my first kiss from this strikingly dark-complexioned, tall guy, a sense of tingling weakness traveled through my legs and bladder at the same time. I felt waves of excitement and trepidation as we walked into an area thick with bushes off the path leading from Lyssons Beach—towards a spot far into the foliage where we could hide from public view. There, he pulled me as close as possible to his chest. His embrace caused my bladder to swell from the anticipation and excitement of our very first kiss. His breathing got louder. I became so exhilarated that I peed myself! Hearing the trickling sound hitting the sand below, he looked down with a sly smile. Afterward, he gave me my first seductive, passionate kiss that I had been so eagerly waiting for.

Even at that age, I knew I wanted to have a meaningful, love-infused relationship. I did not want just lustful moments that would dissipate into faint memories after our adolescent adventures were over. I knew that I wanted to invest my innocence in love.

Love is one of the most abundant energies in the universe. The more love we share, the more it multiplies. Love flows through the energy of affection we give and receive. It influences the decisions we make about those feelings. I hope that everyone gets to experience romantic love at least once in their lifetime.

Love guides our choices. The who, what, where, when, and how we choose to share our affection is totally up to us. The strength of our love, quality of our life, and level of commitment in our service determine how our love stories will unfold. They direct where our journeys will take us and where our destinations will end.

Love shapes our past, present, and future. My mother's love nurtured me with such kindness and care that it motivated me to achieve a greater level of conscious, empathetic love and kind living for her, myself, and others in the world. Throughout my life, I saw my mother demonstrate caring love to family, friends, and total strangers without asking or expecting anything in return. Her spirit of nurturing love has influenced my energy of the compassionate care I now give to her as Alzheimer's hijacks her brain and jumbles her cognition. Multiplying from the love she poured into me as a child, I cultivated a bountiful garden of nurturing, romantic, and empathetic love; that consistently inspires compassion for others while blooming gifts of love. Good gifts always multiply and grow. Love shared with someone will always multiply into nurturing, romantic, or compassionate energy. How are you sharing your gifts of love?

True love is authentic; it's at the core of who we are. Like the heart (organ) within our body, love orchestrates the flow of positivity and goodness in our thoughts and throughout our life. Authenticity gives power! It gives the power to respect, appreciate, accept, and value ourselves and our partners. From my experience, in-depth research, and discussions with partners in relationships, I have found that the three most important components of an authentic committed relationship are love, trust, and communication. These foundational tenets are intertwined in the emotions, feelings, and behaviors that we demonstrate and reciprocate as partners and spouses.

LOVE
- ❀ Nurture
- ❀ Care
- ❀ Appreciation

TRUST
- ❀ Honesty
- ❀ Harmony
- ❀ Security

COMMUNICATION
- ❀ Respect
- ❀ Sex
- ❀ Boundaries

THE GIFT OF COMMITMENT

*Authoring an awesome adulthood requires taking
the initiative and being intentional.
It isn't just going to happen.*

— Brett & Mary McKay

Our wedding day! The day I dreamed of for years finally arrived! The day we legally committed to each other was a beautiful and cool island-vibes Saturday afternoon in August. I was officially committing to the one man that I would devote my life and love to. The man I invested my innocence with was making an official commitment to me. I was elated that we were both committing our romantic love to each other. He was committing to me, his chosen woman, in the presence of our family and friends. I was the chosen one. But chosen for what? Just as the Jamaican national motto says, "Out of Many One People," would I be the only woman (out of many) for him from this day forward?

The thoughts and meanings of our vows to each other became lost in translation. The simple, intimate, small-budget ceremony of this exciting day would translate into different meanings for us. For me, after "claiming" his last name seven years earlier while in the seventh grade, I ecstatically thought, "I finally get to legally be Mrs. Wife." For him, our wedding ceremony translated into including that there would be many more women, but I would be the one who legally has his name, the "one" he builds a family and creates a homelife with. As the spiritual leader the Dalai Lama says in book *His Essential Wisdom*, "True compassion is not just an emotional response but a firm commitment founded on reason. Therefore, a truly compassionate attitude toward others does not change even if they behave negatively. Through universal altruism, you develop a feeling of responsibility for others: the wish to help them actively overcome their problems."[1]

Using the power of our minds—the most determined, computational entity within the human psyche—my husband and I both projected our conscious and subconscious meaning of commitment into the life we desired both inside and outside the relationship. We were validating the basic pillar of the *marrsing* concept: the thoughts that emanate from each partner's level of consciousness will ultimately determine whether it fuels, ignites, or ruins the relationship.

Commitment is a gift! Marriage is a gift! Our relationships are gifts! Gifts are valuable treasures and worthwhile experiences. These are life experiences that some are still looking, waiting, dreaming, or wishing for.

The "I do's" we state at our wedding ceremony build on the foundation of the commitments we promise to each other as a part of our basic marriage pledge: for better, for worse, for richer, for poorer, in sickness and in health, until death do us part. We make the choice to commit our love, life, and passion to each other and to provide emotional, financial, physical, and mental support to our partner through the ebb and flow of life. But keeping those vows and commitments sacred can be challenging. Throughout the years, I believed my vows were for my full lifetime. I now accept God's guidance for a different path towards a new journey. I paraphrase Proverbs 16:9 of the Bible: "Our heart plans our ways, but God directs our steps." We just have to trust that his higher power will continue guiding us onto the right path. Being able to stay committed through decades was an immeasurable gift!

WEALTH IN RELATIONSHIPS

Any act of appreciation affirms our connection to each other. Validates us. Expands who we are in the world. Deepens our spirit. And can turn an ordinary moment into an extraordinary, peachy, and praiseful day.

— Oprah Winfrey

There is wealth in having harmonious relationships and marriages whether it is being committed to that special person through the norms of society or as a legal commitment. There is unique and valuable wealth in being committed to another person through love and dedication. Like any investment we engage in, we can either win or lose. Psychologist Dr. Shannon McHugh says, "It's important to recognize that no one is on the same life path or trajectory. We cannot compare where we are in our journey to others, as we will never feel fulfilled or happy with the process. Focusing on your own goals and how to get there can help us to get out of the spiral of jealousy that often comes with comparison."[1]

Investments are risky ventures, but we must understand that the results depend on how we manage our investments. To accomplish that, we first have to understand the value of what we are investing in and then determine and state the expectations of that investment. We must know how averse we are to risk and how much we are willingly and confidently investing. We need to understand our level of tolerance and our threshold for losses and gains and decide at which juncture we will extract and savor the remaining value of our assets. And we have to acknowledge and bring awareness to the indicators that drive our decisions to divest and reinvest in other relationship portfolios.

Our relationships are investments of love, time, and *self*. Knowing how much we are willing to comfortably lose for the cause will empower us. Oprah Winfrey shares in her book *Words That Matter: Everyday Truths to Guide and Inspire*, "When you're standing there taking your vows and wearing your beautiful white dress, few will tell you that you're entering into one of the most challenging agreements of your life. It's true that a great relationship can help you reach your highest potential. But it's also true that getting there is about much more than romance."[2] In my personal experience, investing more than thirty years in a relationship resulted in a wealth of returns in assets and liabilities. Choosing to find the lessons in our undesirable outcomes equips us with an expansive growth mindset that will take us to the next level in life, love, and relationships. The way we move forward in life is how we repurpose our accomplishments and our disappointments. Our interpretations of our successes and failures develop inside of us and manifest in how we live and love as we move forward.

Love is one of the most valuable energies that transcends the world. It does not belong to any one specific ethnicity, religion, culture, community, society, or nation. It is the ruling emotion that dominates our human existence, and we get to freely share our love with whomever we choose to connect with emotionally or otherwise. Helen Fisher, anthropologist and author of *Anatomy of Love*, shares with us that the effect of romantic love on our brains is similar to an addiction, lighting up the same areas of the brain as cocaine or nicotine. She writes, "Romantic love is a survival mechanism as crucial as the craving for water … this drive, this survival mechanism is also an addiction."[3] She offers a biological and physiological explanation for my requisite dedication to the first man I excitedly married and was romantically in love with for the majority of my life. From the time I befriended him during childhood, I fixated my dreams and aspirations on creating a life-long love journey with him. I was richly blessed with children, and I created many precious family relations and valuable friendships along the way. I also uncovered an invaluable wealth of knowledge while embarking on the quest for understanding how this great romantic love—one that germinated at the youthful age of thirteen blossomed into a family of 3.1 offspring, grew into a marriage of more thirty-one years, and inspired admiration from others—disintegrated into such raw and antagonistic emotions.

We get to navigate our life outcomes by tapping into God's power. An experience this impactful, one about a beautiful, "mishandled" love and the unacknowledged hurt that remains hidden below our life experiences, has an inherent lesson for so many other partners and spouses in the world. By first being consciously aware of God's command of the universe and His presence in our lives, we learn not to lean on our own limited understanding, but instead trust in His higher power to guide our actions. Acknowledge that, as human beings, we are inherently prone to make bad and unlikely choices. This is an important reminder as we navigate the chaos in the world. Instead of allowing ourselves to falter in our life journeys without any universal guide, we must consciously trust in the spirit of God to direct our paths. With the strong belief that God holds all of humanity in his hands, we can gather the treasure of experiences—both good and bad—to help create our next journey. We can save ourselves from losing the wealthy returns from our commitments as we go through times of instability, insanity, and disharmony. We can discover valuable elements amid challenging circumstances. We will find the remains in the surrounding rubble and broken pieces. Sometimes we have to experience pressure to unveil the nuggets of gold, precious diamonds, and beautiful pearls that we are as individuals.

Marrsing Thought

True matters of the heart are not for sale,
they cannot be bought or sold, they can only be exchanged.

Angella Watkis Francis

CHAPTER 4

THE MARRSING JOURNEY—LIVING, LOVING, SHARING

All thoughts which have been emotionalized (given feeling) and mixed with FAITH, begin immediately to translate themselves into their physical equivalent or counterpart.

— Napoleon Hill

Without love we could not survive. Human beings are social creatures, and a concern for each other is the very basis of our life together.

— The Dalai Lama

When I got married at the tender age of twenty, I was overzealously in love. If my husband had offered me a twist tie as an engagement ring or wedding band, I would have gladly taken it with excitement! Just as I envisioned years earlier about getting married to the man who would pick me as his prize, my aspirations were manifesting into reality. I was ecstatic about getting married to the love of my life. More than thirty years later, the details of our small wedding ceremony are still vividly ingrained in my memory.

As an earlier testament of my love for him, I had boldly carried around my "husband-to-be" picture pasted on my schoolbag. I directed my thoughts toward the day we would get married. I envisioned the life and children we would create together as a family.

On my wedding day, as my sister was applying my makeup, I was thinking about how this day had been part of my intentional journey. My dream of becoming Mrs. Francis was finally manifesting. My life aspirations were aligning with my intentions.

I made a commitment to myself to be the best wife I could. Not a perfect wife, just the best that I could be. But to achieve this level of commitment, I needed to invite God into the midst and keep Him there for guidance.

Throughout the years of our marriage, and as we matured into our own individual *selves*, I constantly wrestled with a myriad of feelings and opposing dichotomies of emotions. As we grew together through life stages, the changes in our living, loving, and giving took different forms and expressions.

In retrospect, we both had big egos that we expressed differently. My ego made me sensitive to negativity, cheating, disrespect, and deception while still remaining feisty. The human ego is like a thin but tough layer of skin. The problem with ego is that it gives a false sense of protection and thinks it can protect us from hurt and pain. It is a superficial cloak.

Whenever we get upset or frustrated, the egotistical human side of us wants to first respond with sharp words and explosive emotions, even adding in a few colorful expletives. And sometimes an "eye for an eye" mentality gets thrown in.

The God-powered side wants us to be understanding and forgiving. God-inspired decisions give us power. Our choice to follow the ego of the human *self* or the God-inspired *self* is determined by the quality of our emotional health in the love, life, and service we share in our relationships.

I remain in constant gratitude to God for allowing me to enjoy the manifestations of my desires and aspirations as a devoted partner, wife, and mother. My commitment to become the best wife meant always including the three of us. I chose God to be my third ever-guiding spirit in our relationship and truly depended on God and His powers to fulfill my aspirations throughout my life. I shared love and served in ways that were pleasing to both God and my partner. In return, my ego wanted to be loved and appreciated. I learned that true human love is obligatory. If we sincerely love ourselves first, before loving a partner, we can care, share, and accomplish the extraordinary without forcing or demanding reciprocation.

Our actions and words must align with our purpose: the ultimate outcome we want to achieve. Our relationships and marriages get their qualities from the love, intentions, and level of service that each of us brings to them. Each of us exist as a single person with differing individual energies vibrating from within our spirit. Whether we get legally married, mutually committed, or remain single, we are individually responsible for being our best at living, loving, and sharing. As couples who share intimate chemistry, our vibrational auras change in both frequency and levels depending on our mental, physical, and psychological states. We also share and affect each other's vibrational auras. When we absorb or generate negative emotions, they block the flow of positive energy through us. Raising our consciousness helps us control the energy we put out into the world and the energies we allow to enter and flow through us. As we tap into our *marrsing* energy, we begin to check our state of awareness and ask ourselves what kind of energy we are injecting into our intimate relationships. What kind of love energy will we bring into our future relationships?

God puts love in our hearts so we can share it with others. He commands us to become givers of ourselves in service to each other rather than takers of what we can from our partner. God takes care of what we need when we serve others. Once we begin to trust Him to provide all our needs, we do not have to worry about losing what we have. Giving and sharing is seeding. Planting seeds means we are generously adding to what others have and, in turn, multiplying what we will receive directly or indirectly. If we want to be loved, we must first love others. If we want kindness, we must first be kind.

Intentionality envisions a definite purpose on an authentic path. Authenticity unveils our vulnerabilities. Being vulnerable means acknowledging our pain and traumas in order to heal ourselves emotionally, physically, and mentally. Healing ourselves allows love to grow and bloom within us. It creates a positive path for good energy flow and brings with it the possibility of living intentionally so we can experience peace in our minds, hearts, and spirits. It allows us to have an abundance of good spiritual and emotional energy that satisfies our individual needs and still leaves us enough to share with someone else. Love has a multiplying effect. So, when we share love, we are essentially creating a ripple effect of love sparks that will eventually kindle greater flames of harmony and intimacy. Sharing also adds the multiplying effect of inspiring our partners to be generous. We receive much more from the universe when we become a medium of flow. Through sharing, we learn and grow from exchanges of energies, through wisdom, and by understanding each other. Word of Faith Family Worship Cathedral in Austell, Georgia, is an interdenominational ministry founded in 1991 that is thriving with more than 20,000 members. Founder and senior pastor Bishop Dale Bronner shares, "Never stop learning because life never stops teaching."[1] Every moment in our relationships and marriages offers a learning opportunity to know more about each other. If we are not being consciously aware, we will miss these valuable lessons.

Today, we can begin enhancing and transforming the rest of our lives, marriages, and relationships. Author and spiritual teacher Eckhart Tolle writes, "The power of now can only be realized NOW. It's not about the time or effort. It only requires us to remain actively present in welcoming this moment as it is."[2] We can begin in this very moment to set our intentions toward creating the marriage and relationship that we want with our partners by defining the purpose, unlocking our power, and awakening our passion. Here and now, we can start our *marrsing* mission and embark on an intentional journey to transform the way we live, love, and share with our partners.

Marrsing Thought

Healthy, Harmonious, Successful relationships and marriages are not about GIVE and TAKE. They are about SHARING and SERVING.

Angella Watkis Francis

CHAPTER 5

THE MARRSING ENERGY— PURPOSE, POWER, PASSION

Your intention is to live on purpose.

— Wayne Dyer

No effort can be said to be ORGANIZED unless the individuals engaged in the effort coordinate their knowledge and energy in a spirit of perfect harmony.

— Napoleon Hill

As a child, I understood the power of the mind, the intentionality of our thoughts, and how they can manifest into what we want our life to be. Happy or sad, rich or poor, loving or hateful, abundant or paucal, victor or victim, we have the power to control our emotions and the thoughts we allow to rule our minds, despite our physical environment or any temptations to engage in behaviors that are out of our character.

My tenacity and zest for an intentional life played out at an early age. As the thirteen-year-old girl flirting with this experienced, older boy who later became my husband, I knew how I wanted to engage in physical connections. So, even though I became infatuated with his charm, I remained consciously aware of his ultimate goal. He was patiently courting me because his intention was to pick "my prize of innocence."

Ultimately, he did get me as "the prize and the package" with all the great contents. It happened when I was ready and willing to accept the possible outcomes of my actions. We have the power within us to align our actions with our intentions toward the goals we want to achieve. We will have challenges along the path of life and in our relationships, but they are supposed to strengthen us, not break us.

I grew up in poverty but never felt poor. I never saw my mother express defeat, despite the economic struggles she endured raising me and my siblings. She was a devoted, hard-working, single mother who has inspired me with her poise and calm while navigating her life's journey with faith and trust in God. The inner strength and tenacity she demonstrated inspired me to develop my own tenacity and seek out gratitude in all my experiences.

Reminiscing on some profound moments, I remember one morning she handed me thirty pennies (*30 1* cent coins) from her coin jar to cover the cost of my morning ride to school. Those pennies were all my mother had at the time during her unemployment period, which meant there was no money for lunch that day. She promised to have a meal ready for me after I walked the three miles back home after the school day ended. Missing school was not an option. Even though she only attended school up to the ninth grade, she understood the value of formal education and how it would enhance our future. This "penny experience" highlights my spiritual number pattern with the numbers three and one and has been a lasting model for not allowing obstacles to stop my aspirations. Inspiring me to look for the opportunities from my challenges.

My mother showered us with love, care, and devotion. Instinctively, she filled us with pride, ambition, and motivation so that we believed success is simply waiting for us to grasp it. Through my indelible childhood experiences of recognizing her God-powered perseverance, I learned that being poor is a state of mind. It makes us focus on what we do not have instead of being open and staying aware of all the abundance that exists in this world and in the universe for us to have and enjoy. We must understand that the world holds unlimited resources, and our thoughts should be limitless in imagining the life and love we want to relish. As a result, I have chosen a life path of continuous gratitude and contentment. I constantly strive for success in what I want to achieve, while being consciously aware that God will provide and direct me toward all that I need. If we apply this similar approach to our intimate commitments, we will be rewarded with contentment and harmony.

My physical and socioeconomic environment did not keep me from being happy. It became a contributing catalyst of being grateful for simply being alive. I never developed a sense of envy for material things or for the lives others were living. My mother continuously instilled integrity in us. With her Jamaican patois accent she would always say, "Don't 'red yieye' fi people tings, cause yu wi tief." Translation: "Don't be envious of other people and their possessions because you'll become greedy and steal." Instead, work toward what you want and share what you gain along the way.

We are all uniquely valuable in our own special ways. We just need to uncover and heal our true, authentic *selves* if we want to enjoy harmonious relationships. Rather than looking for a mate with qualities on the superficial list of physical features—cute, sexy, tall, dark, handsome, muscular, brown eyes, blue eyes, blond hair, curly hair—we should choose a partner by assessing their heart, mind, and spirit. We must not leave the physical realm of living on this earth without discovering and sharing our gratitude, uncovering the potential within us and finding out what lies in the universe for us.

In her book *Daring Greatly: How the Courage to Be Vulnerable Transforms the Way We Live, Love, Parent and Lead*, research professor at the University of Houston Graduate College of Social Work and author Brené Brown says, "Vulnerability is the birthplace of love, belonging, joy, courage, empathy and creativity. It is the source of hope, empathy, accountability, and authenticity. If we want greater clarity in our purpose or deeper and more spiritual lives, vulnerability is the path."[1] When we know the value of who we are and the gifts we bring into this world, we can cultivate our own sense of appreciation and begin to understand our life and its meaning. Reaching this level of acceptance, knowledge, and higher consciousness gives us the strength and determination to live wholeheartedly.

Love relationships influence our rational, analytical minds. To get the most out of *marrsing* and enhance and transform our thoughts, actions, and behavior, we have to develop a risk-taking mindset. Our relationships are investments of our time, energy, and emotions. Investing is a risky endeavor. When we begin a relationship, we are sharing parts of ourselves in hopes of increasing and improving who we will become. The odds are that we may lose some or all of our contributions. We must still try to open our hearts and allow the great equalizing energy of love to lead our thoughts and actions through the relationship journey. Regardless of our status in society—rich, poor, famous, CEO, president, or queen—in order to truly experience love, we have to risk some level of openness to truly feel, share, and accept it.

Actively living brings us life's most rewarding and fulfilling moments. We have no control over the details of our birth or the number of years we will accumulate before our spirit and body disintegrate and take us from this existence. The years, months, and days between the moments of birth and death are ours to craft with the choices we make, the thoughts we entertain and the actions we take, resulting in the flow of our life energies through us and out into the universe. Within the laws of attraction, we draw in what we want by asking for it, then aligning our energy and actions toward receiving our request from God and the universe. To paraphrase Brazilian novelist Paulo Coelho from the underlying philosophy of his book *The Alchemist*, the universe will conspire to give us what we faithfully ask for when we put action behind our faith.[2] If we want peace, joy, harmony, comfort, and understanding in our relationships and marriages, we cannot send out anger, vengeance, betrayal, deception, or any other contradicting emotions and actions. Life is all about sowing and reaping, giving and receiving, contribution and retribution, action and karma. It starts with us and our intentions. No matter what the physical world is handing us, we have the ultimate choice and power to choose how we will honor and treat ourselves, our partner, and our relationships. Striving to live actively with positive intentions through *marrsing* will make our relationships great!

Marrsing Thought

Life is best lived when we are maximizing our opportunities with intentionality.

Angella Watkis Francis

CHAPTER 6

"I AM"—THE ENERGY OF MY ENVIRONMENT

You are either contributing to or contaminating every situation and circumstance in which you are involved. It is time to find out which of these you're doing, and how and why you're doing it.

— Dr. Phil McGraw

Life is about patterns; the universe is about patterns. Winners have consistent patterns of constructive and ambitious behaviors. Losers have habitual patterns of destruction and self-sabotaging behaviors. Our environment shapes who we are.

— John Assaraf

Exodus 3:14 says, "I am who I am." The phrase "I am" is one of the most powerful and definitive expressions of our individual strength, belief system, and self-esteem. It originates from what has been deposited within us throughout our lives. It becomes the objective expression and the demonstrative level of our conscience and individual awareness. It shows our acknowledgment and understanding of our *self* as the singular entity who is sharing in God's great universe by being in flow. Austrian philosopher and neurologist Viktor Frankel says, "people forgot that often it is just such an exceptionally difficult external situation which gives man the opportunity to grow spiritually beyond himself."[1] We must use the strength of our mind to repurpose the devaluing experiences of our lives into investments of growth, value, and wealth so we can create love that is authentic and true. This kind of love helps us see past negative behaviors and look for positive traits.

We are a product of our inherited family traits, our environments, and our experiences. These dictate our individual life's blueprint and, in turn, govern our feelings about ourselves. Our feelings shape our beliefs and our beliefs manifest into our convictions. Ultimately, these influences determine the mindsets, worldviews, and individual perspectives that show up in our beliefs around relationships and commitments. These perceptions reflect the way we feel about ourselves and how we tolerate and accept others. They are revealed and reflected in the "I am" statements we express about ourselves: I am beautiful, I am ugly, I am a failure, I am successful, I am smart, I am stupid. These statements frame our inner thoughts and tell others and the universe about our core beliefs, the lens we use to view our environment, and how we frame the experiences as the picture of our life.

When we are emotionally, spiritually, and physically well (healthy), our "I am" statements reflect wellness and positivity. When we are emotionally, spiritually, and physically unwell (sick), we emit bad energy and negativity. We unconsciously live out our "I am's" as we speak, act, and exude what is inside of us. When we are full of negative emotions, our fight energy reaches such a high level that we start searching for someone to fight with or something to fight about. The state of our "I am's" contributes to the harmony or disharmony that exists in our relationships, homes, and intimate environments.

Our home and living environments should be places of positive energy that encourage romance as well as renew, replenish, and re-energize us. The energy of our home is created by the people who live there. The energy we have bottled up inside will appear in our words and actions amid our family interactions. They will permeate our living environment.

Whenever we have disagreements within the home, we should still be able to take time out and re-engage with love, respect, and appreciation toward each other. Negative emotions generate negative energy. Positive emotions emit positive energy. If we have anger inside us, that is the emotion that will appear. Similarly, if we have love inside us, it will flow out as loving words and actions.

Life experiences are multifaceted and leave good and bad memories that ruminate within our minds. Everything we experience affects our energy and vibrations. The internalization of life events forms our perceptions and shapes who we are, ultimately influencing the kind of partner we are.

Marrsing encourages us to take an introspective look into the inner workings of our minds and our behaviors toward our partners. What is at the root of the emotions ruling our behaviors? Where did these emotions originate? Are they coming from childhood experiences, heritage, or cultural traditions? Are we willing to make changes toward enhancing and transforming ourselves? Dyer writes, "When you're inspired by a great purpose, everything will begin to work for you … When you feel inspired, what appeared to be risky becomes a path you feel compelled to follow … Essentially, if you don't feel love, you don't feel the truth, and your truth is wrapped up in your connection to spirit."[2] *Marrsing* is about being inspired to fulfill a great purpose. To do that, we must examine our lives so we can understand and manage our emotions within the context of our relationships, living environments, and marriages.

We must awaken our rational thoughts to uncover, acknowledge, and understand the value we carry in us for our partners, spouses, and the world to enjoy. To purposefully live out our true value, show our unique love, and express the innate sharing of ourselves in service to our partners, we must first clear out the psychological, emotional, and mental obstructions within ourselves. We can start by tapping into our subconscious mind to uncover the blocks and work on releasing our flow.

Marrsing Thought

*Having a wholehearted '**singleness**' plays a major role in having a healthy and harmonious relationship.*

Angella Watkis Francis

PERSONAL POWER

Power (man-power) is organized knowledge,
expressed through intelligent efforts.

— Napoleon Hill

You are today where your thoughts have brought you;
you will be tomorrow where your thoughts take you.

— James Allen

When we create thoughts from our knowledge, wisdom, and the spirit of God, we empower ourselves to understand our life and relationships on a much deeper level. It gives us the ability to navigate our journeys with blessed assurance that when we are weak, God will be strong for us. That is the inner power that we have.

Napoleon Hill writes, "Power is organized effort. Success is based upon power."[1] The quality, duration, and magnitude of our success will be in proportion to the strength of our personal power and our organized effort toward the goals we want to accomplish.

I married for love and a life of togetherness. As a teen, I fell head over heels in love. Being married for more than thirty years has brought with it a myriad of life celebrations and challenging experiences. Each year has enlarged my sphere of gratitude and tested my faith, fidelity, and devotion. In the beginning, I vowed to be devoted through the ups and downs. Later through the years, I prayerfully hoped that the ride would smooth out and become less bumpy as we cruised into the years of maturity. Through this commitment, I learned that falling (in love) and cohabitating on opposing vibrational levels and conflicting powers can weaken and hurt us. When we hurt, our energy gets depleted, and we begin to function below our positive energy level. Low-level energies invite negativity and disharmony.

All human beings emit energy. In his book, *The Eight Pillars of Prosperity*, James Allen writes, "Energy is the working power in all achievement … It is the basic element in all forms of action … Without a considerable degree of energy, therefore, there will be no moral power."[2] Our life and health are profoundly affected by whether energy is flowing freely or sitting stagnant. Our energies are part of our well-being and should be part of our self-care routine. The universe is made up of energies that are constantly being exchanged, transferred, and transformed. Just like universal energies, our relationships are constantly shifting with our thoughts, actions, and vibrations. Aligning these shifts with the desired outcome of the commitments we vowed to keep tests the strength of our personal power on an ongoing basis. Each test strengthens or weakens us and eventually binds or loosens our commitments.

Being consciously aware of our internal and external energies increases our individual power to manifest our progressive intentions so we can achieve our purpose and find harmony in our lives, relationships, and marriages.

Being in touch with our soul puts us on the path toward genuine spirituality. Genuine spirituality means being consciously aware of the energy we are sending out into the universe and the energy we are allowing into our spirit (soul). What energies are we holding onto in our minds, bodies, and souls? What emotional energies are currently blocking our flow?

Living intentionally, loving consciously, and sharing generously with God's guidance and protection is integral to the manifestation of our goals and godly blessings in our lives and relationships. Once we truthfully and genuinely trust God to control and direct our thoughts, actions, and life paths, we begin to see and accept disappointments and failures as obligatory aspects of our life's journey and purpose. James Allen states, "You are the thinker of your thoughts and as such you are the maker of yourself and your condition. Thought is casual and creative and appears in your character and life in the form of results. There are no accidents in life. Both its harmonies and antagonisms are the responsive echoes of your thoughts. A man thinks and his life appears."[3] When we are living intentionally, we manage our thoughts and the resulting emotions. We also monitor our energy levels and energy flow on a consistent basis, to ensure we are not holding on to negativity. If we are, then we should process and replace it with positivity.

As our spiritual ruler, God takes charge of our lives and directs our thoughts. We have to trust that He will offer us strength through challenges and growth from changes. Believing that whatever is happening in our lives is part of His plan, helps us become more highly conscious selves and partners.

Once this is acknowledged, we save ourselves from being tossed around emotionally and psychologically by the turbulence of the physical world.

As God's spiritual followers, we are commanders of our physical existence through His spiritual awakening in our minds. As our consciousness grows, we develop awareness toward the energy that we put out into the world and the energy that we allow into our thoughts and intimate spaces. Acknowledging God as the ultimate power source frees our minds from the mental limitations that hold us hostage in states of negativity and lack. When we awaken the God-force in our lives, we feed our spirituality. We begin to exercise control over our thoughts through guidance from our own inner convictions. We start leading our lives, relationships, and marriages with greater intention and with a higher level of conscious awareness. This higher level of consciousness increases our reverence to God and His profound influence in our lives and in the universe around us.

Living a Godly life does not mean we are perfect or that we will never do things we later regret. Living Godly means that we exist with an ever-present consciousness of His laws, His power, His will, and the universal concept of planting and reaping. Whatever seeds of thoughts we plant and grow will bear the fruits of thoughts we act on. Living a Godly life means we become leaders of our own thoughts and the actions that follow, rather than following a lost and disoriented mind.

In his book *The Soul of Leadership: Unlocking Your Potential for Greatness*, Deepak Chopra explains, "We exist to give of ourselves, and we can only give from the core where our true self exists."[4] To reach our core and transform our relationships, we have to practice *marrsing DIG*(ging). I will explain *DIG* in a later chapter of this book.

Do we know what God's will is for our life? Could we be surrendering too soon? Are we mistaking the disappointments along life's journey as our destination rather than a redirection?

Finding and pursuing our true purpose will ultimately elevate both our minds and level of consciousness. The universal and biblical understanding of God's will in our lives empowers us to discover our unique gifts and intertwine them into our relationships and life dreams. We will gain a true understanding of God's power and the universal ability we have to dream and act toward the future we want. There is a sense of true buoyancy in recognizing the value of being authentic with ourselves and our partners. We can effortlessly discern how our aspirations are positively or negatively affected by the energy of each other and the environment around us. As we gain greater understanding, we acknowledge that God will always direct the powers within the universe to align and yield the most appropriate circumstances for us. The fruits of rewards will manifest as harmony through blessings and positivity in our lives. Harmony emanates from our thoughts, actions, and the vibrations that we generate. It expands outward to meet the capacity of our imagination and the size of our dreams and efforts.

Marrsing Thought

Empowerment is Happiness.
Power is controlling our thoughts: Not allowing our
thoughts to take us aimlessly where the 'others' are going.

Angella Watkis Francis

SOWING SEEDS

*Relationships are based on
four principles: respect, understanding,
acceptance and appreciation.*

— Mahatma Gandhi

*But this I say: He who sows sparingly
will also reap sparingly, and he who sows
bountifully will also reap bountifully.*

— 2nd Corinthians 9:6

Ralph Waldo Emerson said, "We know that the ancestor of every action is a thought."[1] The seeds of someone's imagination, idea, or notion are what manifest into reality. For example, everyday appliances such as washing machines that save us the physical exertion of hand washing, as well as clothing brands and technological innovations, all started from someone's thoughts. The creators dreamed and worked toward making them a reality. Everything was a thought first, then a decision, and then an action toward the goal of creation. Our thoughts create the seed that develops into the individual we are and the partner we become when we commit to another person. Everyone and everything that has impacted our lives are seeds. We are the seeds in our marriages and committed relationships. Seeds need the appropriate elements to grow and thrive. Therefore, we need to feed ourselves positive, productive thoughts if we want to have thriving relationships.

We get to control our own thoughts, feelings, and actions. We are responsible for what we bring into our committed relationships and marriages in the form of energy, emotions, harmony, or disharmony. Positive thoughts generate after we accept, understand, and fully trust God to direct our thoughts and paths. It is then that we will experience peace in our hearts and wisdom in our souls to unendingly overcome any emotional pain, fear, or anxiety generated from our individual hurts.

The seed of change begins with one thought. *Marrsing* is a seed that sprouts our interpersonal challenges into opportunities that enhance and transform the harmony and synergy within our committed relationships. The seed begins to manifest through one single thought, one single life, one single love, and one single dose of compassion at a time.

Dr. Arun Gandhi, cofounder of the M. K. Gandhi Institute for Nonviolence, explained Mahatma Gandhi's work this way: "Gandhi's work in nonviolence was comprehensive and not simply confined to politics or human rights. It was about building positive relationships based on respect, understanding, acceptance and appreciation ... to eliminate disharmony."[2] The seeds of our relationships will only germinate and grow if they are in nutrient-rich environments of respect for each other, understanding for our opposing views and influences, acceptance of our differences, and appreciation for our authenticity. Our relationships also need constant nurturing, attention, and care to continue growing and thriving.

Our prior relationships are seeds. Sometimes we will need to prune the old influences that sprout into branches of inappropriate habits to make room for new perspectives and enhance our *self*. We were born from the seeds of our parents and their actions. My first husband was the seed that grew my romantic love, sprouted my nurturing love for him and our children, and kindled the compassionate service I devotedly shared during our marriage. His seed spurred growth in my transition from a teenager to a woman.

All these seeds encouraged my growth and maturation that led me to understand myself and recognize God's divine uniqueness in myself and in others. Seeds of knowledge about the universal energy flow in my spirituality grew, as did an awareness of the abundance of God's will for my life.

My commitment to our union resulted in seeds of wisdom that allowed me to fully engage in living purposefully, loving powerfully, and enjoying the abundance of the universe. For marriages and relationships to flourish, we need to provide the right soil for growth (intentional living), the appropriate nutrients (conscious loving), and the required attention and care (generous sharing).

On our journey of life through the universe, we will experience challenges and successes, satisfaction and disappointment, victories and defeats, and both happiness and sadness. Be open to it all. It is part of our destiny. We must continue to do good deeds and sow healthy seeds, regardless of the condition of the soil we find ourselves in. Every thought that we act on equates to planting seeds for our own harvest in life.

Our thoughts dictate how we act toward, talk to, and treat each other through our service. Author and former radio talk show host Earl Nightingale says, "We all need each other for water, for shelter and most importantly for love. However, whatever we seek in rewards we must first gain in service to others. Our rewards in life will always match our service because we reap what we sow."[3] The sowing starts in our thoughts.

In their book *Boundaries in Marriage*, self-help authors Dr. Henry Cloud and Dr. John Townsend state, "The functional part of marriage deals with the 'doing' aspects of the relationship, such as paying bills, managing family schedules, cooking meals, keeping house, and rearing children. In the relational aspect of marriage, sowing and reaping is how partners and spouses affect and impact each other's heart with serving and sharing."[4] Galatians 6:7 offers guidance on the spiritual principle of sowing and reaping. This version of God's law of attraction applied as *marrsing* to our relationships simply means that our actions toward our partner contribute to the resulting environment. When we are loving and responsible, our partner will draw close to us. When we are unloving and irresponsible, they will withdraw by shutting down emotionally, engaging in avoidance, and eventually leaving the relationship. Harmony from within sows the thoughts and actions that emanate from our deep inner *self*. By choosing empowerment rather than defeat, and perseverance over vengeance, we can join the *marrsing* mission and begin planting and nurturing the seeds for transformation.

Marrsing Thought

Use the Power of MARRSING to improve our communications. Elevate our minds, Interrupt the caravan of negative thoughts and disembark from the train of destructive thoughts and behaviors.

Angella Watkis Francis

CHAPTER 9

BEING IN FLOW

Don't lower yourself to the ground
to engage in a chicken fight.

— T. D. Jakes

For God has not given us a spirit of fear,
but of Power, and of Love and of a sound mind.

— 2 Timothy 1:7

Our source of flow starts within our God-powered thoughts. Positive thoughts contribute to our flow. Mental blocks generate negative emotions that lead to quarrels and disharmony. Jamaican reggae artist Bob Marley refers to these blocks as "mental slavery"[1] in his song titled "Redemption Song."

We show respect and appreciation in our relationships and marriages by valuing ourselves and each other. When we accept our partner as a unique individual with his or her own set of positive and negative traits, not the person who we think they should be, then we begin to clear the blocks from our minds. Knowing that we are appreciated and respected conveys the feeling of being authentically loved. Whether it is a nurturing love, romantic love, or compassionate love, the feeling of true, honest love is one of the most universally transformative and enriching connections we can experience. However, we can only give away what we have. If we have respect and appreciation for ourselves, then it will easily flow from us toward our partner. If we have love inside of us, then all its accompanying positive emotions and behaviors will flow from us.

Staying in flow opens us up for receiving possibilities and opportunities from the universe. Our beliefs begin in our thoughts. Our thoughts will either open us up for growth and expansion or kill our spirit and stunt our progress. Limiting beliefs keep us from enjoying the abundance of God's earth and the universe. Possessing an expansive belief allows us to soar with expectations for good, better, and best in our relationships and in life.

Our energy of gratitude unlocks the gate of a limiting mindset. Gratitude guides us toward being consciously aware that we are worthy and valued. As we exchange our commitments in marriages and relationships, energy begins to flow from us to our partners. Ask yourself what kind of energy you have within you now. Is it positive or negative? If we have anger, it and all the associated negative behaviors associated with it will flow from us. Negativity, mistrust, hatred, and other destructive emotions within a relationship cause blockage.

Imprisoned in a Nazi concentration camp with little to no possibility of reuniting with his family, Austrian neurologist, psychologist, and author of the famous book, *Man's Search for Meaning*, Viktor Frankel, wrote about surviving the imprisonment experience: "When a man cannot change his circumstances, he should change his thinking about the situation."[2] Holding onto negativity harbors internal blocks that restrict our internal flow of life's energies. Restricting our flow will affect our ability to give and receive the deep emotional love, true romantic intimacy, and genuine compassionate care that our relationships need to grow and flourish. *Marrsing* empowers us to acknowledge and own the who, what, how, why, where, and when of ourselves and our relationships. It elevates our conscious awareness of the energies that emanate from our inner *selves* and the thoughts, feelings, actions, and behaviors that are flowing from the spirit of our inner being into our relationships and marriages.

Consistent negative thoughts and behaviors block our flow of contentment, peace, and harmony. Our ability to give and share depends on our beliefs in ourselves and our understanding of the abundance that exists in the universe. God and the universe will supply all our needs. He told us about this in Psalms 23: "The Lord is our shepherd (provider). We shall not be in want." He will provide all that we need by leading us into green pastures, signifying that there is abundance, growth, and prosperity. He will restore our broken, hurt, and abused spirit. He will anoint our heads with oil to heal us—oil of contentment, harmony, and peace of mind. We just have to take from the infinite source, which is the universal buffet table of God-force love, wisdom, and compassion. Having God-powered love for our partners opens our hearts to flow by sharing and serving compassionately.

Self love cares for our body and soul. Authentic love grows, nurtures, and expands as a positive energy within us. The energy that we put out into the universe comes right back to us tenfold. When we share, we open our arms to embrace. Sharing also means opening up to receiving what others are giving and what God has prepared for us. Psalms 23 says, "He prepares a table before us." Life is a buffet: we can take all that we want and desire. Opening our hearts and hands allows the flow of universal energy and the sense of gratitude, thankfulness, and blessings to reach and ignite each other's souls.

Marrsing is operating at a higher level of consciousness under God's guidance within the context of our intimate relationships and the energies of the universe. It lets us discover the unique individual that we are deep within the sacred level of our being.

Marrsing Thoughts

Use the Power of MARRSING to improve our communications: Elevate our minds, Interrupt the caravan of negative thoughts and disembark from the train of destructive thoughts and actions.

Angella Watkis Francis

CHAPTER 10

THE COMMITTED SELF

*Success is the progressive realization of a
worthy idea [goal]. People with goals succeed.*

— Earl Nightingale

All things are possible to him [her, they] who believes.

— Mark 9:23

What are you committing to as an individual? What are you committing to in your relationship and marriage? Each of us should define the purpose and success of our own life as a guide and the goals we are progressing toward. We receive strength by standing in our own individual power—strength that helps us understand our value and our unique qualities. If we do not know who we are, then we are leaving ourselves open for someone else to define us. Every individual should be able to stand within the God-force power that created us and declare who we are before engaging in a committed relationship. If we do not recognize our true worth as a person, we will never acknowledge our worth as a partner.

Understanding and appreciating ourselves first means discovering and being in gratitude for who we are as an individual. It is empowering to know and understand the value we contribute to our relationship and the world we live in, both as a single individual and as a partner. All of us inherently possess powerful inner conviction to navigate and direct our own paths through life. When we commit to another person, we sacrifice much of who we are as an individual because we will begin to question and rationalize how our individual decisions will affect our partnership. Sacrifice does not mean losing who we are. It means evaluating our decisions from a spiritually conscious perspective. It requires us to step out of our human *self* and include the spirit of holy guidance in our decisions. Having God at the helm and in the middle to guide and direct our thoughts and actions will inspire us to think, act, and behave at a higher level of consciousness.

Each of us is responsible for the individual we are in this world. The choices we make in our lives may be influenced by someone or something else, but it is our own internal thoughts, decisions, and ultimate actions that determine the harmony or disharmony we experience and endure in our relationships. Ultimately, it is within the mind of the single individual that the decision is made to commit, stay committed, or end the commitment. How are we measuring the success of our commitments in our relationships? What does a successful relationship look like for you? Ecclesiastes 3:1 says, "To everything there is a season, a time for every purpose under heaven." Not all relationships are meant to last for a lifetime. What is important to understand is that there is a lesson for growth, change, and understanding in every relationship. The lessons may just be the strength you gain from the experience. Both the individual and the committed *self* should always seek and understand the lessons so we can be grateful for the wisdom.

Marrsing Thought

God is the creator of this phenomenal universe;
he beautifully created the single individual we are
and the committed partner and spouse we'll become.

Angella Watkis Francis

CHAPTER 11

MARRSING VIBRATIONAL ENERGY

Live if you want to live, yeah, positive vibrations, yeah, positive /
That's what we got to give/Got to have a good vibe.

— Bob Marley and the Wailers, "Positive Vibration"

POSITIVE VIBRATIONS

As partners, we bring our vibrational energy into each other's space. Respecting and appreciating our partner creates a good vibrational aura in our homes and marital beds. Being intimate is an energy infusion exercise. No one wants bad energy being transferred from their partner to them. In his book *The Strangest Secret*, Nightingale says, "We don't become rich by diluting others. No man can get rich unless he enriches others. So, we must sow rich seeds to get rich harvest. Our rewards in life; whether in the short term or the long term, will always match the vibrations we generate."[1] As we communicate and interact with each other, we have to be mindful of the damaging words and negative behaviors we display and tolerate within our relationships. Instead of diminishing the uniqueness and originality of each other, we should take time to be grateful for our partner.

Becoming aware of how our actions and vibrations affect our partner is integral to creating a harmonious relationship and enjoying a *marrsing* life. When we operate in unison with God's guidance it means we will be in rhythm with the synchronous vibrations and energy flow of our threesome partnership. We will instinctively serve without expecting a direct return from what we share. It will free our minds from an ego-fueled mentality of "you must 'do' for me what I have 'done' for you." You will not waste time and energy waiting for payback.

The good deeds we do in life go out into the universe and multiply before they come back to us. We have to acknowledge that our partners are not responsible for what the universe gives us. We are. When we share and serve, we are obeying God's will to be of service. Therefore, we get to claim any resulting manifestation of abundance in our lives in the form of peace, joy, and contentment.

Idiosyncrasies are part of our unique, original design from God the Creator. We have multiple facets to our personalities, various quirks, and differing behaviors. Some have amazing spirits of kindness and peaceful auras. However, it is our individual level of consciousness that determines our tolerance and acceptance of another human being who does not share or possess the traits that we deem admirable.

As we become aware, we begin to realize how our emotions affect us and how our individual uniqueness shows up and plays out in our relationships. *Marrsing* helps us to consciously manage our intentions toward what we say and do in matters that affect our interpersonal connections and interactions between ourselves and our partners.

Sometimes God shakes things up to create change and make improvements in our lives. Tony Evans, creator of the Urban Alternative Podcast and founder of Pastor of Oak Cliff Bible Fellowship in Dallas TEXAS says, "God creates crisis in our lives to reveal himself to us."[2] When God wants to reveal Himself at a higher level, He puts us in situations with no other option but to trust Him to bring us to a deeper level of experiencing Him.

When we choose to live a *marrsing* life, we become intentional with our thoughts and actions. We begin to contemplatively align our behaviors with our life aspirations for our marriage and relationships. What we put out always comes back. Send out good vibrations if you want good vibrations to come back to you. Good *marrsing* vibes lead us to more synergistic connections and optimal universal energy flow.

Rather than trying to mold our partners into who we think is the perfect companion, we have to accept the person for who they truly are. Jamaican reggae artist Buju Banton wrote song lyrics that go, "I want to be loved, not for who you think I am or who you want me to be. Just love me for me."[3] It is through the journey of acceptance that we begin to experience joy within our spirits and harmony in our relationships.

CREATING BOUNDARIES

Boundaries are a function of self-respect and self-love.

— Brené Brown

*Boundaries are about self-control. Boundaries
are not something you "set on" another person.
Boundaries are about yourself.*

— Dr. Henry Cloud & Dr. John Townsend

In their book *Boundaries in Marriage*, psychologists Dr. Henry Cloud and Dr. John Townsend write deeply about responsibilities in marriage: "When boundaries are not established in the beginning of a relationship trust breaks down. Or the marriage doesn't grow past the initial attraction onto real transformation and true real intimacy. They will never reach the true 'knowing' of each other and the ongoing ability to abide in love and [to] grow as individuals and as a couple. This is the long-term fulfillment of God's design."[1]

I have learned and understood how healthy boundaries protect our relationships by providing a moral compass for loving, respecting, communicating, and trusting each other. Boundaries define and protect the sacredness of our commitments in our relationships. While appearing with Bishop Dale Bronner on his *True Talk* discussion program, Christian psychologist Alduan Tartt profoundly stated, "Relationships that have no boundaries or rules will end unfavorably."[2] As each partner crosses the unknown lines of "no-no's," the relationship will begin to mimic a field of "landmines" that erode the harmony every time there is an infraction. Boundaries are about identifying influences that can creep in and clandestinely corrode the trust and stability of our relationships and invite unwelcome guests—such as infidelity—into our marriages and unions.

When partners are devoted and willingly serve and share with each other, the relationship is healthy. However, to serve and satisfy our partners, there has to be mutual understanding of what is acceptable and what is unacceptable within the marriage or relationship. We empower ourselves by setting boundaries between our psyche and the people and things that are beyond our control. Creating healthy boundaries in our lives also means we will not allow sinister behaviors and manipulative partners to dictate our actions or have command over our existence.

Further in their book *Boundaries in Marriage*, Dr. Henry Cloud and John Townsend caution that, "Having [or creating] boundaries in marriage is not about fixing, changing, or punishing your mate. If we are not in control of ourselves, the solution is not learning to control someone else. The solution is learning self-control. It is more about taking ownership of our own life so that we are protected, and we can love and protect our spouse without enabling or rescuing him or her."[3] They further note, "Responsibility tells us we are the ones who must work through our feelings and learn how to feel differently. Our attitudes—not those of our spouse—cause us to feel distressed and powerless. How we behave and react is part of the problem and we have to change these patterns. We allow ourselves to get pushed beyond certain limits and then become resentful or powerless."[4] Therefore, we need to acknowledge our individual value and own our power so we can make conscious choices that align with our intentional journey and purpose.

Giving in to temptation can lead to discomfort and even suffering. Boundaries have been a part of our existence from the beginning of time. Genesis 3:3–4 talks about God setting a boundary for Adam and Eve not to eat from the one specific tree in the garden of Eden in order to protect them. He allowed them the freedom to eat off any tree except the forbidden tree. God was not controlling them; He was protecting them and future generations. He was protecting the future from the maladies that follow if we yield to temptation.

The Dalai Lama teaches us that freedom is not the opposite of boundaries. In his speech titled, *Non-Violence, the Appropriate and Effective Response to Human Conflicts*, he says, "[Human] conflicts do not arise out of the blue. They occur as a result of causes and conditions, many of which are within the protagonists' [and antagonists'] control."[5] Each of us are protagonists in our life story and we will inevitably become antagonists if we do not communicate and respect what is important for our relationships to thrive in harmony.

Drs. Henry Cloud and John Townsend also note that, "God designed the entire creation for freedom. We're not meant to be enslaved by each other;

we were meant to love each other freely. God designed us to have freedom of choice as we respond to life, other people, to God, and to ourselves [and the universe]."[6] Within each of us as individuals, we carry the greatest power that all humans possess: the freedom to choose. But when we turn away from God's guidance, we make choices that end up harming our lives and our relationships. As a result, we become enslaved to sin, self-centeredness, other people, guilt, and other harmful dynamics. Boundaries strengthen our self-control. Listen to how Paul tells the Galatians (5:1) to set boundaries against any type of control and become free: "It was for freedom that Christ set us free; keep standing firm and don't be subjected again to a yoke of slavery." God tells us to not be subject to any kind of enslaving control.

Psalm 23 guides us in acknowledging that God's will for us is to trust Him to restore our souls and heal us. He wants us to be obedient and follow Him as the guiding force in our life so He can fill us with goodness. When we follow our God the shepherd, he gives us what our hearts desire. He will satisfy our wants, deliver us from the things and people who are harmful to us, and lead us into the house of the Lord with a life of blessings.

We should tap into our God-source through prayer and meditative introspection. The Lord's Prayer in Matthew 6:9–13 is, "Our Father in heaven, hallowed be your name. Your kingdom come, your will be done, on earth as it is in heaven. Give us this day our daily bread, and forgive us our debts, as we also have forgiven our debtors. And lead us not into temptation but deliver us from evil." This prayer encourages us to call on God to help us create boundaries from temptation and protect us from immorality so that His will for our destiny will manifest in our lives.

All relationships require work and dedication to maintain the intimacy within them and respect the boundaries that our commitment establishes. The strength of our connection depends on how we feel about each other and how we handle both the negative and positive actions of one another.

CHAPTER 13

OUR RIGHT TO CHOOSE

It is in the quiet crucible of your private personal suerings that your noblest dreams are born, and God's greatest gis are given in compensation for what you have been through.[1]

— Wintley Phipps

Between stimulus and response there is a space and, in that space, lies our freedom to choose.[2]

— Stephen Covey

The behaviors we consciously or subconsciously engage in will affect our character and interpersonal relationships. If these behaviors are fed by negative and destructive thoughts, they will ultimately cost us emotionally, mentally, spiritually, and financially. They will eventually ripple outward and destroy valuable family structures and meaningful relational connections.

The ability to choose is a personal right that we are born with as part of our existence. Our actions flow from our thoughts. Therefore, no matter what happens in the physical world, we have the right to choose what we do with our thoughts, actions, and experiences.

When we become consumed by negative reactionary emotions like anger and resentment, it affects our mental capacity to make wise choices. The Dalai Lama shows his prudence when he states, "Under the power of anger or attachment we commit all kinds of harmful acts—often having far reaching destructive consequences. A person gripped by such a state of mind and emotion is like a blind person who cannot see where he is going. Yet we neglect to challenge these negative thoughts and emotions that lead us nearly to insanity."[1] We must find healing for the pain that weakens us into losing our God-power within. The longer any of our emotional trauma remains unresolved, the more it will end up controlling us. Trauma will evolve into destructive habits that ruin us. These clandestine habits will begin operating as demonizing behaviors that secretly infest the foundational structure of our minds and then our relationships.

Life encapsulates the span of years between the moment we take our first breath in the world to the moment we take our last (natural) breath. John Kehoe shared the following insightful statements:

"Keep your conscious mind busy with the expectation of the best, and make sure the thoughts you habitually think are based upon what you want to see happen in your life. Water takes the shape of whatever container holds it, whether it be in a glass, a vase or a riverbank. Likewise, your mind will create and manifest according to the images you habitually think about in your daily thinking. This is how your destiny is created. A new life is created by new thoughts."[2]

Each day we wake up and are gifted with a new twenty-four hours to accomplish all that we hope, wish, and pray for. How we choose to use these twenty-four hours within each living day is a part of our individual power and free will.

We will all have good and bad experiences whether we are married, committed, or single. Allowing past experiences to negatively dominate and dictate how we treat ourselves and others is not living well with intentionality. Stephen Covey writes, "Disappointments are inevitable, but misery is a choice."[3] What are you doing with the lessons you learn from your disappointments?

DECIDING TO CHANGE

*Your subconscious accepts what is impressed
upon it with feeling and repetition whether
these thoughts are positive or negative.*

— John Kehoe

Be transformed by the renewing of your mind.

— Romans 12:2

Transformation is about first understanding and believing that the individual *self* is susceptible to the many weaknesses that are inherent in all humans, then working towards the "next level" to our greater *self.* Worry and happiness cannot occupy the same heart at the same time, so one has to leave. *Marrsing* offers a path for choosing your happiness. It provides wisdom in our decision-making and transformational understanding of how to accept our truths, direct our energy and intentions, and own our relationship journeys.

Understanding that we need to rely on a higher power to face and conquer the negative forces that can derail and disrupt our lives is important in effectuating lasting change. Reaching toward the positive elements of life allows us to live abundantly with intention, love more consciously, and share with greater compassion and generosity.

The power of *marrsing* guides us in replacing the negative thoughts with positive ones. It is about empowering ourselves and raising our consciousness about our behaviors in order to ultimately change our thinking and enhance our relational connections. It gives us valuable wisdom to handle our everyday interactions within our relationships.

A good place to start is by acknowledging the supernatural spirit of God in our lives. Matthew 6:33 says, "But seek first his kingdom and his righteousness, and all these things will be given to you as well." This means that we can experience peace even when there is turbulence going on in the physical world. If we carry around all the experiences that we encounter in our lifetime, it will equate to tons of weight dragging us down.

Sometimes we remain attached to old relationships, past friendships, or individuals who have hurt, betrayed, or disappointed us. This takes up valuable space in our hearts and minds in the form of toxic thoughts. If we carry around toxic thoughts, they will permeate our well-being, produce negative emotions and reactions in our communications with our partners, and cause emotional contamination.

Again, I share one of my favorite verses from the Bible, Proverbs 3:5–6: "Trust in the Lord with all our hearts, do not lean on our own understanding." We must acknowledge God in everything that we think and do. We must have a dialogue with Him about our thoughts and actions and let Him direct our path. If we truly believe in His higher power and allow Him to lead our lives, we will learn to appreciate the good times as well as the bad. The ebb and flow of life is part of His predestined path for each one of us.

During a conversation with my youngest son he profoundly said, "Mom, heavy things don't fly." That is, if we are constantly being burdened by the weight of the disappointments and misfortunes in our lives and troubles of the world, we will never soar to a higher level of living. Months later, my son also shared the analogy that songbirds sing more often when they are feeling comfortable, happy, and well and not as much when they are experiencing discomfort. How much unnecessary weight are we carrying around that is burdening us and limiting our power? How much discomfort are we enduring that is discouraging our singing?

The baggage of our past can keep us stuck. We cannot move lightly when we keep the heavy things within us. The birds of the air soar freely through their lives and enjoy the wind beneath their wings because they are not carrying burdens. Burdens prevent us from achieving our aspirations, hopes, and dreams. The heavy weight of unresolved issues uses up our positive energy and constricts the expansion of our imagination that could otherwise manifest greater good in ourselves, relationships, and family. It clogs us up with the debris of negativity and limiting beliefs from our past disappointments, hurts, pains, and traumas.

Bishop T. D. Jakes says, "Too many of us live our lives and relationships as chickens rather than eagles."[1] Too often we are unwilling to embrace the opportunities of using our wings to become better versions of ourselves to improve our relationships. We need to tap into our inner power of tenacity and courage to help us let go of our past victim mentality. We must let go of our outdated, false traditions that keep us pecking around on the ground—like chickens waiting for our demise of becoming hot wings in buffalo sauce.

Being actively engaged in the possibilities and opportunities of life can be like an eagle flying. *Marrsing* power encourages energy to flow through us and out into the universe, and it allows that power to consciously receive and release the energies of the universe so it can be regenerated and reciprocated. Flying opens great opportunities for the exploration of unknown possibilities to enjoy in unsurpassed harmony. Pastor T. D. Jakes shares, "Chickens are just fine pecking around on the ground for their food source and survival while eagles pursue their goals and purpose—gliding through the air looking for new opportunities and undiscovered food sources. Chickens live a limited existence while eagles live in the abundance of the universe. Chickens criticize the eagles for soaring."[2] When we value ourselves, we understand that being called demeaning names by our partners is because they want to devalue, bully, and abuse us. We should not allow our partners to clip our wings with their criticism and stop us from soaring into our purpose. Partners must support each other's dreams and aspirations if they are going to soar together.

Bishop T. D. Jakes further advises, "We should live our lives with faith, courage, and dignity. Don't dumb down our integrity by getting into a chicken fight when we are eagles."[3] As eagles, we do not have to defend our choices. We proudly own the decisions that we make in concert with God's words and direction to embrace our destiny!

The force of *marrsing* empowers us to focus on the source rather than on the symptoms of our misaligned actions and disharmony. While driving to work on January 5th, 2016, I heard a "Thought of the Day"on Connecticut's WIHS radio station: "When we put our problems in God's hands, he puts peace in our hearts." This thought has truly inspired me and is now a mantra in my life. Being worried, irritated, or frustrated about the innate behaviors and idiosyncrasies of our partners is disempowering both to us and our relationships. Remember, some of these behaviors and characteristics that now threaten our relationships were the same ones that gave us butterfly feelings when we first met our partners. It is our interpretation about the behavior that has changed.

CHAPTER 15

MARRSING DIG = DEEP INNER GRATITUDE

*Your thoughts are the primary creative forces
in your life. Use them consciously and use them
often and you will awaken to a whole new life
of power and opportunity.*

— John Kehoe

Brain scientist and author Dr. Jill Bolte Taylor paraphrases Einstein in her book *My Stroke of Insight:* "You have to leave who you are in order to become who you want to be."[1] For her, it took a literal health stroke to bring her to this state of realization. We should not need to suffer such life-transforming health challenges to begin enhancing and transforming ourselves toward experiencing harmony in our relationships. We can use the power of *marrsing* to accomplish that.

Imagine the wheels on a bicycle. If even one tire is flat, the bicycle cannot move forward smoothly. The same can be said of a relationship. Each person in a relationship is like the wheels on a bicycle. Both need to be operating at full capacity and be in sync and harmony in order to move forward.

Living a *marrsing* life allows us to discover and understand our power to change, control, align, and direct our emotions and actions. This allows us to elevate ourselves to a higher level of consciousness and ultimately toward building synergistic relationships.

THE INNER PERSON CHECK-UP

Let's start by doing a *Marrsing DIG*—Deep Inner Gratitude—that will identify the baggage we bring into our relationships. We can then hand it over to God, leaving it in His grace and power. Give God the heavy issues and situations through "prayer handoffs." Start developing a trusting relationship with the all-powerful God of the universe and let Him be the director of our lives.

The *marrsing DIG* is both a precheck and an ongoing checkup of our emotional baggage and overall well-being. The more life experiences we have, the more baggage we accumulate. The heavier our baggage, the harder it is to authentically connect with someone and soar with them. The baggage carried over from childhood, trauma, family division, abandonment, and feelings of inferiority, taint our vision of greatness and will continue to weigh us down. As Stephen Covey writes in *Living the 7 Habits: The Courage to Change*, "Our history is behind us and our potential is ahead of us."[2] Use the *marrsing DIG* to get ready for potential relationship journeys that will open the possibilities of harmony on our *marrsing* mission.

Let us dig inside ourselves to invoke the memories of childhood experiences and identify how they connect to the current patterns in our adult life. Licensed counselor and clinical supervisor Tracy Smith writes, "In the early 1960s, behavioral psychologists began fleshing out attachment theories. They argued that parental rejection powerfully influences children's thoughts, feelings and behaviors."[3] Go deep within and travel down memory lane and remember the level of nurturing that we received. Let us ask ourselves, "Do I feel valued? Were my childhood experiences happy or sad? How did the makeup of my household and family dynamics influence my views on how a spouse should be?"

In order to have healthy marriages and relationships we have to heal the *self* first. Our secrets follow us and will eventually become psychological, mental, and emotional burdens. We are responsible for our own healing and what we bring into our relationships and marriages. We have to be emotionally healthy and spiritually fulfilled to allow true love and all the abundance of the universe to flow through us. In her book *Rising Strong* Author Brené Brown says, "Of all the things trauma takes away from us, the worst is our willingness, or even our ability, to be vulnerable. There is a reclaiming that has to happen."[4] Taking that first step to acknowledge and heal the painful experiences of our past starts with a brave and vulnerable *DIG*. Vulnerability allows us to become confident enough to take the emotional risk to share with our partners what we have been through and seek their support in helping us deal with our trauma monsters.

It is people who make the world. If people remain hurt, broken, sad, angry, jealous, and vindictive, then the world will reflect those negative emotions and emit that same energy into the universe. Mark 7:15 says, "Nothing outside a person can defile them by going into them. Rather, it is what comes out of a person that defiles them." Mark 7:23 states, "All these evils come from inside and defile a person." We must *DIG* deep inside our subconscious to find the true *self* buried beneath our public persona.

We have to work on processing the repressed memories that clandestinely rule our thoughts and feed our fears. We are all leaders of our lives. In his book *The Soul of Leadership*, Deepak Chopra talks about developing our spiritual intelligence—the part of our consciousness that makes us more aware of our thoughts, behaviors, and interactions with others. As we acknowledge our partners and their personal history, it helps us to be mindful. Consider this statement from Chopra: "Everyone is acting from his or her own level of consciousness; however hurtful someone is, he/she is doing the best they can, given the limits of their consciousness."[5]

When two individuals take the time and effort to deal with the blockages—past hurt, lingering pain, emotional trauma, disappointment, and failure—the two people will release and discover all the lasting value they have hidden beneath the blocks.

As we become more consciously aware of how our thoughts and emotions play out in our behaviors, we are inclined to think about the value of our love and the wealth of our committed relationships. Did our childhood experiences increase our value or shrink our spirit down to negativity? What do each of us bring to our relationships? How much value is given to our history, heritage, and experience? How much will they contribute to or cost the relationship? Are we valuing or devaluing our marriages and relationships with what we have inside us? Some of us are carrying around undiscovered treasures and repressed emotions that will eventually show up to either develop beautifully or erupt destructively.

We are responsible for taking care of our individual energy flow. But how do we address the negative behaviors that manifest from our internal dialogues? Whether we are coexisting as committed partners or as legally married couples, we have the individual freedom to choose the thoughts that will elevate our minds or dampen our spirits. We must unearth who we are as individuals and understand what feeds us, starves us, or energizes us. Part of evolving into our authentic *self* is becoming emotionally, mentally, and psychologically healthy. The path to a healthy mind begins with healing from within. It is about being able to uncover who we truly are beneath our ego, shame, and pain. It means having the strong desire to upgrade our *self* to a higher version and taking the time to deal with our suppressed emotions.

We have to take the time to deal with our past trauma emotionally and psychologically. It is only after we have identified, acknowledged, and owned our history and experiences that we will be able to master the effects of our past and whether we will let them disturb and regulate our psyche. We think we can keep our past and secrets hidden forever, but they will manifest into addictive behaviors and expose themselves in our character, lives, and relationships. As a popular saying goes, "Whatever is in the well will come up in the bucket," meaning that what is deep within will certainly show up in our personality. We must take the time to privately take care of our issues before they become public embarrassments.

WE HAVE GREATNESS WITHIN: DO THE DIG

We cultivate harmony in our relationships by planting seeds of honesty and authenticity—honesty within ourselves with a willingness to discover, reflect, and own who we are. Our transformational journey starts with uncovering the authentic *self*. This journey unfolds the inner story of who, what, why, when, and how the threads of our experiences, relations, and cultural influences weave the fabric and create the temperament (the individual *self*) of who we are as a partner or spouse. A *marrsing DIG* helps us discover what pains us, heals us, and feeds us from the inside. Author Richard Rohr says, "If we don't transform our suffering, we'll transmit it. Hurting people end up hurting other people."[6] Carrying unresolved pain and suffering is heavy and weighs down our spirit and body. At some point we will end up unloading it onto our partner. Dumping our pain and suffering onto our partner causes misery and creates disharmony.

A *marrsing DIG* uncovers what is buried within us so we can be our authentic *self*. We might be pleasantly surprised when we find the treasures we have within us. As we acknowledge what haunts or motivates us, we unlock the potential to accept and care for ourselves and ultimately align our purpose with our intentions. A *DIG* into who we are on the inside will open our hearts and minds and show us our gifts and shortcomings so that we can love with greater awareness.

Doing *DIG* exercises elevates our consciousness and unlocks the compassion within so we can understand our value. If we do not know our worth, we will not understand the significance and value that we are bringing to our relationships. Uncovering the true person within us awakens many emotions and takes us through some possibly painful and challenging memories, but it will be rewarding. We have to discover our inner *self* before transformation can begin. Taking a deep dive within ourselves helps us recognize our value. To recognize our *marrsing* transformation, we have to know where we are starting from so that we can chart our journey towards achieving our goals and ultimate purpose.

DIG(ging) begins the acknowledgment of our authentic inner *selves* and the experiences that paint the portrait of our lives. It identifies the thoughts, perceptions, and beliefs that empower us to achieve and helps us begin to choose the thoughts and actions that align with the true purpose of our intentions. A *DIG* raises the level of our consciousness as we become more cognizant of our emotional state and well-being. Accordingly, it increases the generosity of our compassion as we understand the abundance of the universe.

STEPS FOR A MARRSING DIG

There are seven integral steps to conducting a *marrsing DIG* so we can discover what influences, motivates, or frustrates us.

1. **Identify, Acknowledge, and Own the True Person Inside:** Examine our nurturing, childhood and life experiences, and family dynamics
2. **Declare, State, and Reiterate our** personal **I AM** statements that we created from our worthiness introspection and reflection activity
3. **Acknowledge our Influences and Beliefs:** People, places and cultures contribute to who we become
4. **Identify and Express What is Desired** from our relationships and marriages

5. **Identify and Express What is Important in Life Right Now**
6. **Identify and Express Who is Important in Life in the Next Five to Ten Years**
7. **Discuss the Differences:** No two humans are alike

CHAPTER 16

GRATITUDE FOR GREATNESS WITHIN

We have a lamp inside us, the lamp of mindfulness, which we can light anytime … We can produce the energy of mindfulness and return to the awakened wisdom lying in each cell of our body.

— Thich Nhat Hanh

Our lives are shaped and influenced by many factors, individuals, and circumstances. They influence and affect us both consciously and subconsciously. Sometimes we experience life together (siblings, for example) but do not end up with the same influences or perspectives. The nurturing we receive, our perspectives on life circumstances, and our family dynamics all contribute to the true inner person we are. Our interpretation of our earlier experiences plays a definitive role in our connection and communication in our relationships. Brené Brown shares, "That childhood experiences of shame change who we are, how we think about ourselves, and our sense of self-worth."[1] We must uncover the sources of what, where, when, how, and why our thoughts form roots and grow. We must allow ourselves to become vulnerable enough to face our deepest fears and threats.

WHO AM I? IDENTIFY, ACKNOWLEDGE, AND OWN THE TRUE PERSON INSIDE

As children, we are innocent beings dependent on the adults in our lives to love, nurture, and protect us. Adults who abuse and disadvantage innocent children should carry the heavy burden of their bad behavior, not the children they hurt. When we become adults, we are responsible for taking care of ourselves and healing any pain inflicted upon us when we were helpless children. This includes the sometimes uncomfortable and difficult task of seeking help and taking the necessary actions to heal the brokenness, abuse, or dysfunction that we experienced as children.

We have to acknowledge and process those life experiences that have impacted our well-being and perceptions. By owning our truths, we get to study and fully live with our history rather than being controlled by our past. If we do not face our fears and own our stories, someone else can capture them and use the details as weapons to scare and hurt us. I understand that dealing with the brokenness and regrets of our lives takes courage and effort, but owning our history prevents the past from haunting our spirit or demonizing our character secretly and publicly.

Unless we *DIG* deep within our life experiences and uncover our truths, we will not be able to honor and own who we truly are. It is imperative that we recognize, acknowledge, and deal with each and every one of the impactful events that occurred in our life. Unprocessed issues and situations in our past will continue to ruminate in our minds. They will hijack our thoughts and haunt us at the most inappropriate times, roaring and threatening our sense of self-control and self-worth.

An article from "The Art of Manliness" website posits that, "The human story does not always unfold like an arithmetical calculation on the principle that two and two make four. Sometimes in life they make five, or minus three."[2] This helps drive home the importance of examining our past, assessing and acknowledging how our history influences our present and future behaviors.

Author Brené Brown writes, "To love ourselves and support each other in the process of becoming real is perhaps the greatest single act of daring greatly."[3] … "Daring greatly means finding our own path and respecting what that search looks like for other folks."[4] For her final thoughts in the book, she summarized, "Daring greatly is not about winning or losing. It's about courage."[5] Our commitment to our *self* and to our partner must include a "safe space" to acknowledge, honor, and still love the "hurting parts" of who we are currently, so we can grow into our "better future *self*."

Winston Churchill once said, "Being able to assess reality with completely clear eyes, while simultaneously exercising the capacity to see it romantically, is a rare, but attainable gift … the contact between our different beliefs/ideas/interests creates access to new knowledge and planes of existence that wouldn't have been possible otherwise."[6] We have so much potential and value within us. We can enrich our lives just by opening up our windows of imagination and begin exploring the great possibilities of the treasures within us.

DECLARING WHO I AM

If we view ourselves as incomplete,
we'll always be chasing what we don't have.

— Pastor Tony Evans

Start saying this statement consistently: "I am the most original [*your name*], daughter/son of [*parents' names*] that exists. You will **never find** another **true copy of me** in this world. I am **valuable!**"

Declare, state, and reiterate your "I am" statements that reflect your inner treasures you uncovered during the *marrsing DIG*. Write seven statements (one for each day of the week) about yourself that are truthful about the inner person you have discovered or reaffirmed from your deep self-acknowledgement work. These statements represent your strongest personal beliefs about yourself. We are the best of who we are simply because we are an original creation. Say out loud to yourself, "I am the worthiest [*your name*] you will ever find in this world."

These statements affirm our individuality and uniqueness as an original design of God. They should express our values and significance as a human being. Each statement must begin with "I am" because it is not a question, it is a statement, an affirmation, a true expression of what we **truly believe** about ourselves.

Many pioneering thought leaders have touched on the subject of "*self*" and discovering our "I am's." Vietnamese monk and spiritual leader Thich Nhat Hanh says, "To be beautiful means to be ourselves. We don't need to be accepted by others, we need to accept our *self*."[1] Another influential author, Neville Goddard, in his book *The Power of Awareness*, writes, "When we say 'I am,' it's a feeling of permanent awareness. Man's concept of himself determines the world in which he lives and his concept of himself in his reaction to life."[2] In the Bible, Joel 3:10 says, "Let the weakling say, 'I am strong.'" This principle should regulate every aspect of our lives, whether it is social, financial, intellectual, or spiritual.

The *I AM Discourses*, a collection of thirty-three religious dictations by spiritual master Saint Germain states, "'I am' is about recognizing our own true identity and purpose in the universe. 'I am' is the reality of understanding when something happens, we must seek out an explanation on the phenomena of life." In 1 Chronicles 17:16, King David sat before the Lord and asked, "Who am I, Lord God, and what is my family, that you have brought me this far?"[3]

Our flaws, talents, and idiosyncrasies make us who we are. We have to own them. We must boldly lift our arms, open them wide in gratitude, and praise and shout our "I am's" in appreciation to God for his unique design of us.

In *Becoming a Leader: How to Develop and Release Your Unique Gifts*, Munroe writes, "When we understand who we really are, we gain a deep conviction about our obligations to humanity and to the life the creator has given us."[4] I believe those who have not yet started the dive deep within to uncover and discover who, what, why, where, when, and how we exist in the world as a unique individual have not yet uncovered the embryo of what is growing inside. We are still filled with our authentic *self*, our wealth of love, our true zest for living, and our universal gifts, all unborn. We are walking around still pregnant with our true inner being and our life purpose undelivered. Let us initiate the birthing process so we can transition into the next phase where we begin pushing through the blockages that are keeping us stagnant. To fully live, we must move from the confining environment and limiting growth capacity of a mere existence and allow ourselves to participate in the abundance of the universe. With all the opportunities that are flowing throughout the universe, let us begin the process of giving birth to our true, authentic *self*.

ACKNOWLEDGING OUR INFLUENCES AND WHAT WE BELIEVE

The deepest and most valuable connection we have is with our "individual *self*." Self-appreciation and self-criticism are all inside of us. In his book *The Power of Your Subconscious Mind*, Joseph Murphy says, "You can bring into your life more power, more health, more wealth, more joy, more happiness, by learning to contact and release the hidden power of your subconscious mind. You need not acquire this power; you already possess it. But you want to learn how to use it; you want to understand it so you can apply it in all departments of your life."[5] We must look within and clean out any old, unhealthy beliefs that sabotage our lives. Bestselling author John Kehoe reminds us that "everything we think about subconsciously or consciously affects our lives."[6] Our life is the mirror of all the thoughts we have entertained and acted on.

We need to acknowledge where our influences and beliefs come from. The people who have touched our lives, culture, family history, and childhood experiences all contribute to shaping who we are. The words of our parents and guardians during our innocent years of childhood will echo in our souls for all our lives. Everyone in our life who has inspired or criticized us still holds a whisper of influence in our adult years—including those who nurtured, ignored, or abused us. Including community and world leaders who inspired us with their leadership, bravery, generosity, or despotism, they all influenced and shaped our personal views of love toward ourselves and the world.

We attract people, circumstances, and relationships that are within our subconscious. I'll reiterate what Kehoe writes in his book *Secrets of The Subconscious Mind: The Easy Way to Create Success*, "Keep your conscious mind busy with the expectation of the best, and make sure the thoughts you habitually think are based upon what you want to see happen in your life. A new life is created by new thoughts."[7] Are you happy with the life and relationship you have? If not, start by changing the thoughts that are dominating your subconscious.

Our influences show up in the recurring patterns in our lives. Kehoe talks about the concept of patterns in our lives, advising us that we should "trust life to give us an accurate reflection of our choices, patterns, and habits, both internally and externally."[8] Our patterns have meanings. They originate from our past situations, heritage, culture, and experiences. They all contribute to our perceptions and influence our thought processes and behavior patterns. Have these influences been hurting or healing us? How are these influences playing out in our relationships? Do we tolerate abuse because the people we loved, admired, and respected either were abusive or endured abuse themselves? Sometimes, without realizing that we are being abused, we carry on with little or no realization of its future effects on our psyche and our future generations.

IDENTIFY AND EXPRESS WHAT WE WANT

When we align our intentions and actions with our purpose, we will have more fulfilling relationships. There must be a purpose for whatever we devote our time, energy, and emotions to. To find the reason behind our dedication, we need to ask some questions: What do I want from this relationship or marriage? Why am I in this relationship? Am I looking for a partner with good parental characteristics, a passionate lover, or a dedicated ride-or-die who will stay until the end? If he or she is going to be a partner for the rest of my life, do we need to be monogamous? What does infidelity mean for each of us? What does cheating look and feel like for each of us? Do the definitions and benefits of being married have the same meaning and value for each of us? How do we view and define a successful and thriving marriage or relationship?

IDENTIFY AND EXPRESS WHAT IS IMPORTANT

Priorities change over time. It is important to determine what aspects of our lives will get the most time, energy, and resources. Ask yourself the following: What am I focusing on for the next three to five years of my life? What are my immediate priorities? Are my current priorities my children, career, or formal education?

Our mental and emotional well-being benefit when we identify and define the most essential elements in our lives during each specific period of our journey and relationships. Is it our health or the ability to provide for and protect our families? Making a physical note of these priorities will help minimize our anxiety and anchor us during life turbulences. Identifying and defining these aspects of our lives means we are creating a boundary to contain the amount of worry we allow in each challenging situation. Our anxiety levels and mental demarcation points encircle who and what we allow to be a source of stress in our lives. This enables us to allocate our love, dedication, time, and efforts effectively when we are facing consuming challenges.

Our priority list may change monthly or yearly, but having a list can protect us from avoidable heartache, wasting precious time, and losing energy and resources on less important issues and individuals. Creating this boundary in advance allows us to make prompt decisions about our priorities and the effective use of our energy and time, freeing up time for the most important and joyful aspects of our lives.

Ask yourself what your long-term goals in life are. What do you hope to achieve within the next decade of your life? What does success mean for you? And I do not mean success from the perspective of your parents, cultural heritage, or societal expectations. Rohr says, "We suffer when we're not in control."[9] We must always take time to determine what success looks like for each of us and envision ourselves on the journey of our individual path of success and relationship outcomes.

IDENTIFY AND EXPRESS WHO IS IMPORTANT

Ask yourself who is important in your life. Who are the people in your life who need you the most in the next five- to ten-year span? Is it your children, parents, siblings?

Our actions of today determine the future of our tomorrows. Our committed relationships connect and support a vast network of family, friends, and relatives. This network can span across a myriad of interconnections and different degrees of separations. Our network influences our lives and our relationships. However, we must not allow our friends and family to rule our committed relationships. It is important to consciously choose who belongs in the inner circle and whose opinions will have value in any decision that affects our relationships. Everyone's opinion is based on their history and experiences. Not all intentions will be in our best interest.

We are the only ones who should make personal decisions about our marriage or relationship status. Whether we decide to end our relationship or continue it, all decisions about our marriage must be aligned with spiritual guidance, purpose, aspirations, and God's will for our lives, not by relatives and friends who may be influenced by their own subjective experiences.

Another person's opinion about our marriages and relationships should remain *their* opinion. Understand that we have the power to accept or reject anything that enters our thoughts. We as human beings have the power to choose, yet so many of us use the phrase, "I didn't have a choice." We always have a choice. We may not like the choices that are available in the current moment or situation, but the capability to choose still remains one of our inherent human powers. We need to decide if we are willing or courageous enough to deal with and accept the consequences of our choices.

DISCUSS OUR DIFFERENCES

The traits that attract us in the beginning of our relationship can frustrate and annoy us later on. As our relationships grow, we will either become stuck in our ways or mature with knowledge and wisdom. We should be sharing our hopes, dreams, and goals with each to align our lives with our purpose.

Marrsing Thought

We must dig deep inside our subconscious to find the true self. The unexplored self, that is buried beneath the repressed memories will quietly begin ruling our thoughts and feeding our fears.

Angella Watkis Francis

MARRSING PAUSE

Let no corrupt word proceed out of your mouth,
but what is good for necessary edification,
that it may impart grace to the hearer.

— Ephesians 4:29

The life which is unexamined is not worth living.

— Socrates

We need a *marrsing pause* to re-calibrate our *self*! To take time out to intentionally breathe and regulate our body to think and act optimally. As partners in an overstimulated society, and with "fear of missing out" (FOMO), we do not spend enough quality time with ourselves to explore our own thoughts. We are constantly on the go or occupied by all the demands and external stimuli in our environment. A *marrsing pause* is intentionally taking quality time to think about our own emotions, feelings, and behaviors and how they affect us and the relationships in our lives. We need to take personal time to introspectively explore our deep inner *self*, our fears, our emotional traumas, and our personal energy flow.

"Between stimulus and response there is a space. In that space is our power to choose our response. In our response lies our growth and our freedom."[1] I first heard this quote on Stephen Covey's audio book, *The 8th Habit: From Effectiveness to Greatness* when he credited Viktor Frankl for the words.[1] However, upon further research for its original source, I found the original being credited to Rollo May, practicing psychologist, psychoanalyst, and a 1948 faculty member at William Alanson White Institute. May authored a publication titled *Freedom and Responsibilities Re-Examined* in which he writes, "Man's capacity to be conscious of what he is experiencing, to experience himself as subject and object at the same time, to be aware of himself as having a world and being interrelated with it. Mind is the individual's capacity to transcend the immediate concrete situation and think in terms of 'the possible.'"[2] A *marrsing pause* extends the space between the words or actions that affect us (stimulus) and the thoughts and actions we generate and display (response).

Our words and actions cultivate or deteriorate our relationships. As committed partners, we can apply the concept of *marrsing* to enhance and transform our relationships and marriages by starting with the individual *self*. This comes from activating the brain's limbic system in the scientific form of cognitive flexibility. Science writer, public health advocate, and promoter of cerebellum optimization Christopher Bergland explains, "Cognitive flexibility represents a person's ability to switch between modes of thought and simultaneously think about multiple concepts while multitasking."[3] So, during our *marrsing pause* we get to redirect, rephrase and reactivate an alternate path for our negative and potentially destructive thoughts. Taking a break to analyze and rethink our thoughts and actions and their effects on our relationships will dramatically change their trajectory. Using a *marrsing pause* to interrupt the train of negative thoughts and emotions raises the good vibrations in our intimate spaces.

A *marrsing pause* allows us to alter and redirect our thoughts and feelings and gives us the space and time between stimulus and response to consciously tap into our rational psyche before we express toward our partner. It helps to prevent destructive and dangerous outbursts. When we take time out to contemplate our next expression or action, we get to create ones that will align with our mutual goals. Using a *marrsing pause* helps us rationally choose and determine whether we want to enhance and transform our relationship or destroy it. The words and actions we use toward our partners will end up nurturing, hurting, or healing them and ultimately the relationship.

Just like our words and actions, love flows from our heart. What is our heart saying to our spouse with the words and actions we express to them? Are the words we utter bringing beauty or ugliness into our relationships? In his book *The Voice of Knowledge*, Don Miguel Ruiz writes, "It is amazing what the word can do. The word creates images of objects in our mind. The word creates complex concepts. The word evokes feelings. The word creates every belief that we store in our mind. The structure of our language shapes how we perceive our entire virtual reality."[4] Let us color our words with respect and appreciation, words that reflect endearing love and beautiful feelings from our heart to our partner's heart. Use the *marrsing pause* to direct your communications toward the goal of experiencing a harmonious and synergistic relationship and marriage. Take a *marrsing pause* to reflect and redirect!

Like any living entity, our love and relationships need to be fed and nurtured so we can continue growing. The Austrian neurologist and philosopher Viktor Emil Frankl, who wrote about his survival experience in Nazi concentration camps is famously credited with saying, "Whatever gives light must endure burning." In his book *Mans' Search for Meaning* he wrote, "Life ultimately means taking the responsibility to find the right answer to its problems and to fulfil the tasks which it constantly sets for each individual."[5] Just as candles burn out and have to be reignited and changed, in our relationships, the feelings of romance, passion, and enthusiasm will also burn out. We need to take the responsibility to reignite our romance and passion by consistently sharing and serving each other in ways that are nurturing. We need to integrate and prioritize the consistent act of renewing our minds and strengthening ourselves and our relationships. Nurturing our hearts and feeding our souls on a consistent basis is integral to living an abundant life. In his song "How Could I Leave," Jamaican song writer and reggae singer Dennis Brown fittingly says, "Love is just like a rose/if we don't water it every morning; the love will wither and die."[6] If we consistently miss opportunities to nurture ourselves and our partners, then our relationships and marriages will be dull and boring. Consistent dullness leads to lifelessness and lifeless relationships will not survive to bear good fruits of passion and romance.

So, take a *marrsing pause* before acting on immediate thoughts. Making decisions that will become permanent on an emotional basis can be detrimental. Use the time during the *marrsing pause* to contemplate on the desires we want to manifest in our relationships and lives and ask ourselves if the action we are about to take will lead to a positive result. Are we confident in owning the outcomes of our decisions? Are we standing for what we know to be the truth? We do not need to defend our Godly choices, we only need to state them with Godly conviction.

The harmony and synergy within our relationships equate to the quality of our partnership. Positive vibrations will increase with the level of care and attention we give to each other. To emerge healthy and strong, we need care. Each of us needs nurturing and protection to evolve into the best potential *self* and partner we can be.

WORDS HAVE POWER

We all have the potential for good as well as bad.

— The Dalai Lama

Thich Nhat Hanh, who was nominated for the Nobel Peace Prize by Dr. Martin Luther King in 1967, is a global spiritual teacher and Zen master who has dedicated his life work to inner transformation for the benefit of individuals and society. He shares, "When we say something really unkind, someone will do something in retaliation and our anger will increase. We make the other person suffer, so they will try harder to say or to do something back to get relief from his/her suffering. That is how conflict escalates."[1]

FAITHFUL AND FEISTY

Fight energy is depleting to the human spirit.

— Bishop Dale C. Bronner

Our beliefs stay with us and become involuntary responses that color our reactions during our communications. During my high school years, I was regularly sent to detention. I received several verbal or physical disciplinary actions from teachers and school administrators for being overly opinionated and feisty. I could not keep quiet when a classmate was being treated unfairly or when there was any situation that I passionately disagreed with. I believed I had the right to express my views along with the brewing emotion that came with them. I carried that feistiness into my adulthood for a period of time until I realized how wounding a sharp tongue can be. I would feel guilty and remorseful after a heated exchange with my partner, so I knew it was not a behavior I wanted to continue. As I matured into a higher level of consciousness and reflected on the aftermath of each quarrel, I learned that winning the war of words meant that we were both losing affection for each other. I had to start thinking consciously about how my behavior was affecting my sense of peace and the harmony in our relationship. I found guidance in Proverbs 15:1 that says, "A gentle answer turns away wrath, but a sharp word stirs up anger." I copied this biblical lesson, then framed and displayed it on our bedroom wall with pictures of us depicting harmony in our relationship. I hung the frame on the wall in our bedroom as an inspirational reminder that being faithful but feisty can still invite disharmony in my marriage.

DIFFERENCES

No two humans are alike. As our relationships grow, we will either get stuck in our ways or mature with knowledge and wisdom. Egos usually occupy the driver's seat during our young adult years. Whenever we think someone is disrespecting us, the egotistical persona instinctively jumps into defensive mode.

Our thoughts would immediately begin steering towards an ensuing battle. We become feisty and say sharp and hurtful words. Then end up feeling deflated afterward for the verbal wounds we have inflicted. Looking back on my marriage, I now realize how our communication differences played a role in how we expressed and shared our emotions.

It is important for partners to discuss their communication preferences at a time of calm rather than during a disagreement. The Dalai Lama says, "The proper way of resolving differences is through dialogue, compromise and negotiations, through human understanding and humility. We need to appreciate that genuine peace comes about through mutual understanding, respect and trust."[2] Circumstances change the reception and meaning of our expressions. Words expressed in moments of calm will have a much different impact if they are expressed during a disagreement or a verbal fight.

When we think we are being attacked we will defend ourselves. Being defensive puts us in the spirit of war. War mentality invites fight energy, both of which contribute to a negative state of consciousness. This negative state of mind encourages defensive words to hang around like extras on a movie set, ready to make appearances in the quarrel scenes. Keeping an arsenal of verbal weapons invites war and contemptuousness into our relationships. It causes us to operate at a lower level of consciousness because we are constantly prepared for reactionary defense rather than being in a state of calm, contemplative reasoning.

Can we remember how many reactionary words were fired as weapons during our last defensive argument? We usually remember less than half of what we say during an argument. But the sharp words our partner hears and remembers can cause unspeakable damage long after the arguing ends. The life and death of our relationships are in the expression of our words; love or hate, respect or hurt, appreciation or abuse all carry levels of positive or negative energy when we use them. Destructive words produce lower levels of energy that diminish our flow and dull our spirit. Words of affirmation raise the level of energy, increase our flow, and brighten our spirit.

As we begin to use our *marrsing* power to enhance and transform ourselves as partners with intentionality, consciousness, and generosity, feistiness will no longer play a starring role in our responses. We will start choosing respectful words rather than hurtful ones because we know that sharp words cut deeper than physical wounds. We can never undo the pain we cause from the sharp, piercing words thrown at each other during heated arguments and angry communications. In the end, we can only speculate on how deeply we have hurt each other.

Words have power. We should be mindful and conscious about the language we use in our relationships—to our partners, spouses, and children. As Psalms 19:14 says, "May these words of my mouth and this mediation of my heart be pleasing in your sight, Lord, my Rock and my Redeemer." As we strive toward living a *marrsing* life, we must work on being consciously aware of the words we use to communicate in our relationships.

Bishop Bronner states, "Never underestimate the impact of words,"[3] and Proverbs 18:4 says, "The words of the mouth are deep waters, but the fountain of wisdom is a rushing stream." Words can be a source of wisdom and so many other things. Hurtful words may not break bones, but they surely break hearts and cause invisible wounds. On a Jamaican radio station, I once heard a profound public service announcement spoken by a child that said something along the lines of, "Sticks and stones hurt my skin, but hurtful words cause wounds deep within." Our words have power! Use them cautiously and consciously.

Invisible wounds leave lasting mental, emotional, and psychological scars for many years because they take much longer to heal than physical wounds. It is important to be mindful of the language we use in our communications, especially with the people we expect to continue to love us after the argument is over. We must think about the effects of our words before we speak them. Curse words and vulgar expressions cut like knives and swords. The invisible wounds that our words inflict can cause irreparable damage and will ultimately destroy our marriages and relationships.

Bishop Bronner cautions us about the impact of our words: "Our choice of language (words) can:

❀ determine direction or cause stagnation
❀ release healing or create wounds
❀ inspire confidence or create fear
❀ convince or deceive
❀ inspire or discourage

❁ bless or curse
❁ affirm or discredit."[4]

Consider taking a *marrsing pause* to contemplate the language we are uttering during our heated conversations, so we do not end up falsely accusing, condemning, or vilifying our partners. We are responsible for the words and actions that we put out into the universe. Let us question ourselves by asking, "Do I want these destructive words coming back to me?"

Hanh offered these cautionary words that I believe apply to our intimate and committed relationships: "When our partner insults us or behaves violently towards us, we have to be conscious enough to see that they are suffering from their own violence and anger. But we tend to forget. Instead, our anger rises too, we begin to suffer, and we want to retaliate and inflict punishment. Then, soon we have anger and violence in us; just as they do. It's only when we see that our suffering and anger are no different from their suffering and anger that we will begin to behave more compassionately."[5] Every action begins within thoughts of the individual *self*. When we look inward for the meaning of our actions, it opens up our consciousness to understanding ourselves and our patterns.

As soon as we begin to reach a higher level of consciousness, we will stop arguing and fighting, especially over inconsequential matters and material things that we cannot take with us into eternity. Instead, we will begin choosing more peaceful resolutions. This means releasing the energy of the disagreement to the higher power of God. He is the great source of peace for our spirit and all things within the universe.

Frequently, it is our thoughts of not having enough that invite a poverty or greed mindset. The feelings of scarcity, plenty, and abundance all flow from our spirit of gratitude. Our level of gratitude shows in our expressions through service and compassion.

American singer and songwriter Stevie Wonder, who has been blind since birth, has a famous quote (that I have not been able to find the original source for) about his mother that goes, "Mama was my greatest teacher, a teacher of compassion, love, and fearlessness. If love is sweet as a flower, then my mother is that sweet flower of love."[6] Stevie's recollection of his mother's words of love and encouragement had a profound effect on his success. Despite not having sight, he did not lose hope in life because words with positive emotions were served by his mother. As parents, guardians, teachers, leaders, or anyone who can influence another person's life, we must take the time to think about the energy of our words and actions before we speak and act. Likewise, with our words, we should consistently work on being a source of positive affirmation for our partners. Take a *marrsing pause* and allow the goodness within us to become infused with scriptures and affirmations to guide our language and behavior, especially when we are angry to the point of irrationality.

CHAPTER 18

CHALLENGES WILL COME

Every failure brings with it the seed of an equivalent success.

— Napoleon Hill

When we are not able to change our situations ...
we are challenged to change ourselves.

— Viktor Frankel

We can dwell on what went wrong,
or we can focus on what to do next.

— Bishop Dale Bronner

God enriches us with relationships, marriages, and the amazing feeling of loving someone in a true and soul-touching way. Offering ourselves to another person through the abundance of the life we live, the love we express, and the gifts we share can make life an extraordinary synergistic journey. But even more amazing is having that level of dedication and service reciprocated with honesty, appreciation, and respect. I am thankful for the experiential matrimonial journey that spanned more than three decades of living, loving, and sharing myself in the energy of love.

God the Divine Ruler guides and protects us along our life path. The positive power of love can conquer any obstacle or challenge we encounter if there is God-force unity between the committed partners, and we have a mutually agreed upon destiny for our lives together. But negative emotions such as hatred, jealousy, and vengeance divide and destroy any union that excludes God's direction and will.

Marriage must be a threesome—spouse one, God, and spouse two—to overcome the interpersonal challenges that are inevitable when different personalities, spirits, energies, and other elements come together. If Godly love is not at the foundation, our commitments will not sustain harmony. Realistically, we have to step out of our human *self* for patience, tolerance, and strength when we are dealing with all the idiosyncrasies of another person while managing our own habits and flaws, especially when it comes to our intimate partners. Sometimes we will get annoyed and frustrated with their behavior to the point of thinking we made a mistake in choosing them.

But are these the same characteristics that attracted us? *Marrsing* empowers us to take a pause and assess our thoughts before we act on our annoyance and frustration. This is when we should breathe, calm our raging emotions, and avoid using the sharp, lethal words that wound our partner's spirit.

A special nonverbal means of communication needs to be created for the times when our weaponry of words and actions starts roaring to join our arguments and damage our relationships. The more heated the interaction gets, the harder it will be to make rational choices. We need to consciously walk away from heated and potentially dangerous scenarios if we want to preserve our relationships. Little pebbles create big ripples. Eventually, the ripples will build and become tidal waves. We have to expect disagreements when two people coexist because no two individuals think alike on everything. A *marrsing pause* is a valuable tool to use to consciously communicate with our partner nonverbally when words are not a good option. Expressing ourselves in a healthy way is critical to having harmony and peace. If we cannot express our emotions and feelings to the ones we are mutually committed to, then we might seek other outlets for our pent-up emotions.

When our relationships reach an unhealthy state in which hateful words are being spewed and both partners do not want to repair the relationship, then preserving the individual *self* should take priority. Hatred does not belong in our relationships; it incites violence and chaos into a sacred environment and can lead to violent crimes.

Practice speaking words of honesty and peace rather than words of war. The key to peace is trusting God to guide our thoughts and actions. As Bishop Bronner says, "Use our mouth as a water fountain and not a blow torch to spit fire."[1] Always keep in mind that words have power. Proverbs 18:20–21 states, "From the fruit of their mouth a person's stomach is filled; with the harvest of their lips they are satisfied. The tongue has the power of life and death, and those who love it will eat its fruits." Our words are either poison (destructive) or fruit (nurturing). We have the power to choose. Saying "I'm sorry" is a nurturing phrase that waters a marriage. "I surrender" is a fruitful phrase that ends the disagreement and war.

Several psychologists have concluded that those who are hurting will hurt other people. Similarly, on the TV show *Super Soul Sunday*, Oprah Winfrey interviewed bestselling author Dr. Gary Chapman who shared, "Under anger is pain and under pain is fear and fear stifles love."[2] Bishop Bronner echoes this sentiment, remarking that "fear feeds our thoughts; thoughts become action and actions become our behavior and behavior defines our character."[3] The *marrsing DIG* will show the valid connection of how our unhealed hurts can fester into characterizing an inner damaged *self* in the form of destructive behaviors that can pollute the emotional environment of our committed relationships.

WHAT MARRIAGE AND INFIDELITY MEAN TO US

*The people who cause us the most pain are our greatest teachers,
it just takes time to learn the lessons from the experience.*

—Pema Chodron, *Welcoming the Unwelcome*

How many of us as partners in our relationships share the same definition of what marriage, love, and infidelity means to each of us? It was after fifteen years of marriage that I finally asked my husband what his definition of marriage was. His response was, "the person who you want to make life and a future with." It was in clear contrast to my definition of, "when you finally find the person you love so much that you want to spend the rest of your life loving, sharing, and caring with and for them." Neither response was wrong. Clearly, our dissimilar perceptions of the same relationship meant that we would value it differently. I was expecting him to use the word "love" in his response. I loved him so much and expected him to be as much in love with me as I was with him. I thought of him as the only one for me. As the years of marriage evolved, I found out I was only one of many "conquests" for him. Why do two people who said the same vows to each other on their wedding day live those commitments so differently?

Each person has the power to choose how and who they will share their love with. The decision to marry usually means "I found the one and I can stop looking," meaning we choose our spouse after much consideration and elimination. Relationship blogger Ellie Delano posted an article in *Woman's Day Magazine* titled " 'Capstone'" Marriage vs 'Cornerstone Marriage' " stating, "The cornerstone model of marriage builds in an expectation of difficulty while partners are building a life together. This model presumes, optimistically, that people are transformed for the better by sticking it out through the tough times. The capstone model of marriage is much less forgiving of sexual betrayal because it presumes that those who finally get around to marrying should be mature enough to be both self-regulating and scrupulously honest. The increased unacceptability of infidelity is one of the many reasons individuals are waiting longer to marry."[1] I see this model as a wonderful opportunity for individuals to invest time *DIG*(ging) within to uncover the values, idiosyncrasies, and influences of who we are. So, when we decide to commit to our partner, we will be able to share our authentic self, honor our commitments, understand our feelings, and value our self-worth.

In her book *The State of Affairs: Rethinking Infidelity*, psychotherapist Esther Perel says, "It is the stories that lead us into the deeper human concerns of longing and disenchantment, commitment and erotic freedom."[2] What stories of your childhood, family, and culture are derailing your relationships and marriages? Have you had any childhood experiences that are influencing your thoughts and behaviors relating to sex, intimacy, and love? How are your life experiences playing out in your role as a partner?

Our vibrational auras and individual energies can collide and dissipate if both partners are not consciously working toward a mutual destiny. If we want to nurture our relationships and marriages, we should be authentically honest with ourselves first and then our partners. Honesty changes the interpretation of our actions and builds trust, which in turn builds and grows relationships. Perel writes, "Marriages based on attraction and love are often more [emotionally] fragile than those based on material motives ... They leave us more vulnerable to the vagaries of the human heart and the shadows of betrayal."[3] When we share love in intimacy, we expect a reciprocal partnership in similar devotion.

All viable and worthwhile relationships and marriages should include an honest discussion of each partner's views and definitions of love, commitment, marriage, and infidelity. Based upon my research on relationships, talking to partners and spouses, and my own experiences, this is how I define love, commitment, marriage, and infidelity:

❁ **Love:** Love is not just a feeling but also a pledge—a pledge to care, protect, and support. When we love, we implicitly pledge to care about how our thoughts and actions affect our partners, and that means thinking before we indulge in any outside sexual transgressions. Take a *marrsing pause* to ask yourself, "Will this action I am about to indulge in be hurtful or disrespectful to my partner?" We pledge to accept the responsibility of protecting our partners from harmful people, situations, and circumstances whenever we can. We also pledge to support our partners in whatever they are experiencing emotionally, psychologically, and physically. This includes sharing in their joy, pain, disappointment, and success.

❋ **Commitment:** Commitment is the pledge we explicitly communicate to one another either verbally or nonverbally. It is the affirmation of love, support, and protection toward our partner.

❋ **Marriage:** Marriage is the official and legal coronation of a committed and intimate love relationship.

❋ **Infidelity:** Infidelity is the outside entanglements, transgressions, and impulsive escapades that one partner gets involved in without the knowledge or permission of the other partner.

How do you define love, commitment, marriage, and infidelity? Does your partner know your meaning and understand the importance of each of these values to you? What are your commitment goals for your relationship?

Perel wants us to consider what infidelity (cheating) means to us and how we feel about it.[4] Many of us define cheating and adultery as engaging in forbidden sex. As a result of our societal and cultural evolution, that narrow definition has been expanded to include other secret indiscretions and dishonest transgressions occurring outside the relationship without our partner's knowledge. Whatever our individual perceptions are about crossing the line, we need to let our partners and spouses know what those boundaries are and how damaging or detrimental it will be to the relationship and marriage if they are crossed.

Lasting emotional connections from outside our relationships and marriages can ruin the sanctity and sacredness of our vows and commitments. Perel says that emotional infidelity was not recognized in earlier generations as cheating.[5] For me, this theory provides a false pedestal that I sat on while wearing my robe of fidelity. In today's society, we hide our infidelities under the disguise of a "friend I enjoy spending time with" cloak.

My experiential analogy of infidelity is that of termites invading the structural wood that firmly stabilizes a house. I did not know when the first termite entered, but as time went on, many other termites entered freely and unnoticed. Increasing in number as the years went on, they continued gnawing at the inner core of the wood of my relationship. At some point,

I noticed one or two wandering around the structure, but I quickly dismissed them as little, inconsequential bugs that are just looking for attention. Then, wittingly, all the termites invaded and weakened the wood from the inside, destroying its inner core until all that was left was broken wood unable to provide the commitment of strength and security for a solid foundation. Eventually, the increasing deceptions got exposed. It went on far too long, and so too much damage had been done by the termites that the structure had to be torn down.

It is not only sexual entanglements outside committed relationships that qualify as infidelity. Perel notes, "There is a whole range of encounters that include varying degrees of emotional intimacy."[6] Establishing an emotional connection with someone outside our relationship can destroy the trust within our primary intimate relationship or marriage. Even if we are simply confiding in or connecting with another person who is not our primary romantic partner, even if no sex is involved, it can be viewed as infidelity.

The American Association for Marriage and Family Therapy (AAMFT) published an article about infidelity on their website that states the following:

> "The causes of infidelity are complex and varied. Affairs can occur in happy relationships as well as in troubled ones. Harmonious relationships hinge on reciprocity, and a prolonged imbalance of give and take can easily lead to disharmony. In addition to low self–esteem, reasons for infidelity include relationship deficits such as a lack of affection, or a social context in which infidelity is condoned.
>
> Multiple affairs may be symptomatic of an addiction to sex, love, or romance. Sexual addicts are compulsively attracted to the high and the anxiety release of sexual orgasm. But such release comes with a cost to his or her self-esteem, resulting in feelings of shame and worthlessness. Conversely, philanderers who perceive sex outside of a long-term relationship as an entitlement of gender or status take advantage of opportunities without guilt or withdrawal symptoms. Frequently the involved partner will re-write the relational history in order to justify an ongoing affair.

Common reactions to the loss of trust, security and shattered assumptions include obsessively pondering details of the affair; continuously watching for further signs of betrayal; and physiological hyper-arousal that can lead to clinical anxiety. The most severely traumatized are those who had the greatest trust and were the most unsuspecting.

[Cheating] shatters the idea and the notion that we are the prized partner with irreplaceable uniqueness. In translation, it's saying, we are easily replaceable. This can be shattering for the partners and spouses who are giving their all to the relationship and consequently expecting all from their partner."[7]

Certified Sex Therapist and sociologist Dr. Marty Klein authored an issue titled *After the Affair ... What?* wrote, "You can't prevent someone from betraying you. They either choose to be faithful or they don't. If they want to be unfaithful, all the monitoring in the world won't stop them."[8]

When our partners and spouses engage in intimate rendezvous with someone else, we feel violated, deceived, angry, and jealous. Infidelity is a thief. It steals the intimacy that belongs within the committed relationship and devalues it. It is an invasion of the intimate space and private moments that we do not want to share with outsiders. As a result of this invasion, jealousy rears its head and begins to roar, sometimes snarling relentlessly.

Describing jealousy, Perel states that it is "that sickening combination of possessiveness, suspicion, rage, and humiliation that overtakes our mind and causes us to contemplate unkind deeds."[9] Jealousy sneaks into our subconscious and wreaks havoc on our emotional state. At times, those contemplative thoughts can be antagonistically sinful toward the guilty parties. In the words of the Dalai Lama, "When we lose control over our minds; through hatred, selfishness, jealousy, or anger we lose our sense of judgement. Jealousy causes us misery and prevents us from progressing [positively] and spiritually. Sometimes manifesting into aggression that eventually makes us want to harm the other person."[10] Once we become aware of the jealousy hijack, we should deal with it as quickly as possible and release it (as hard as it can be). We should not allow negativity to roam around our minds and manifest within our thoughts, actions, or behaviors.

Expanding on the concept of jealousy, Perel writes, "Betrayal is less about love and desire and more about symptoms in need of a cure … An affair simply alerts us to a pre-existing condition, either a troubled relationship or a troubled person."[11] The American Association for Marriage and Family Therapy notes that "while the majority of affairs happen as the result of relational dissatisfaction, they also happen as a result of personal dissatisfaction and low self-esteem [within the individual self, the one having the affairs]."[12]

Loving consciously keeps us aware of the energies that affect us and our environment. Our consciousness will alert us to the presence of negativity and vibrational auras that can distort our communications and cause chaos in our relationships. Cultivating harmony starts with the thoughts we bring into our conscious awareness on a consistent basis. Jealousy and infidelity choke the life out of the love, trust, and communication within our relationships. Once these crucial elements are no longer present in the relationship, they will exist on life-support until either partner decides to "pull the plug" and let it go. Talk show host, motivational speaker, and author of *The 5 Second Rule*, Mel Robbins says, "If it's dead, bury it. When the energy of what we are doing is leaving us, we should leave it and move on."[13] Traditionally, when we get married, our vows are for a lifetime. As time evolves and infidelity, disrespect, and abusive behaviors seep into our relationship, continuing in that destructive lifetime commitment could literally be shortening our lives.

Marrsing Thought

Whether it's our relationship, marriage, sanity,
heart or our mental, physical and emotional health.
If it's important or valuable to us then it's worth
protecting and preserving with the power of marrsing.

Angella Watkis Francis

SHARING AND SERVING IN OUR RELATIONSHIPS

*For us to receive our blessings, we should be open
to giving and receiving. In order to give and receive,
our hearts, hands, and minds should always be open.*

—Pattie Labelle

What a beautiful experience in life it is to share, give, and receive true soul-touching love. Author Paulo Coelho says, "When we love, we always strive to become better than we are. When we strive to become better than we are, everything around us becomes better too. When we are loved, we can do anything in creation. When we are loved, there's no need at all to understand what's happening, because everything happens within us."[1] If we spend most of our time, energy, and resources focusing on what we do not get from our partners rather than what we can offer them, we will miss out on being grateful for the positive aspects of who they are and the reason we initially committed to them. We will fail to recognize opportunities for us to serve and to share who we are as a unique and exceptional partner. We should focus on being the best individual and partner we would want someone to be for us. God blesses us to serve and share with others. If we let God provide all our needs through him, then all we have to do is serve others. Serving is planting. Abundance is the fruit of good seeds. Remember, we can only control our own actions and reactions.

The energy we put out into the universe is ours and ours alone. What we give and send out comes back to us. In the Bible, Proverbs 16:24 says, "Pleasant words are like a honeycomb, sweetness to the soul and health to the bones." This biblical verse is teaching us to use encouraging words in our interactions so we can keep positivity flowing in our relationships. In his book *The 5 Love Languages*, Dr. Gary Chapman says that we should be fueling our partners on a consistent basis by "filling their love tank."[2] This is true even when we do not think our partners deserve it. We must get in the habit of always thinking about the effects of our words and actions.

If we expect fruitful harvests, we must sow positive seeds. Sowing negative, bad, or destructive seeds as a means of justifying our actions (because we think our partners are not behaving well) is not conducive to a peaceful or harmonious relationship or home environment.

Marrsing power is about having good intentions and good actions. When we are intentionally good to our partners, we add value to how they feel and think about themselves. In essence, we contribute to one of the most important foundational needs of humanity—to feel valued. Having someone who cares about us despite our shortcomings makes a world of difference in how we feel about ourselves and how we enjoy life. Even if we are not in a committed relationship with another person, valuing ourselves first is vital to being able to offer worthiness.

Use *marrsing* energy to invoke the universal God-power within and to strengthen us through the relationship challenges that threaten our well-being. Sometimes we need the universe and all its angels to form a strong band of superhuman strength around us so we can continue loving the important people in our lives. We have to step out of our human *selves* and awaken our spirituality in order to appreciate our partners' value. Even when we get frustrated, we should think about our partners' individual worth as a person. Loving our partners and spouses with the love of God is a way toward *marrsing* through those challenging marital situations. In relationships, we have to expect challenges and prepare for them. They are a part of growing together and melding into the unique couple we will become.

We must consistently feed our minds with daily doses of empowering words and affirmations to continually work on heightening our spiritual awareness so we can tap into the extraordinary strength, faith, and tenacity that are abundant in the universe. If we do not get strengthened and replenished consistently, our sense of spirit will diminish, our positive energy will dissipate, and we will become weakened by the storms of life. When we become spiritually and emotionally weak, we rattle and get tossed back and forth by the smallest wind. Over time, weakness diminishes our inner light and erodes our energy, *DIG*nity, pride, and self-worth.

As young children, my siblings and I were ushered by my mother to all the neighborhood religious children services that were being taught in our town. The denomination of the church was inconsequential. If it was a house of Godly and moral worship, there we would be, dressed in our best outfits and ready to have our minds and souls fed with positive and affirming influences. My mother would be right there to take us back home after the children's services ended. Each religious teaching had slightly different interpretations about popular Bible stories such as "Noah's Ark" and "The miracle of the five loaves and two fish." Through these stories I learned to be open to different views, perspectives, and beliefs about the same subject matter as foundational lessons for accepting the uniqueness of everyone in the world.

My mother instilled values of kindness in me as a young child by demonstrating kindness toward others and accepting each person for their different perspectives. She taught me to seek out the value in each religious denomination or sect with a sense of curiosity. All that mattered was that we were learning about God-powered living, loving, and sharing. She was shaping our morality and igniting our compassionate spirit to build our conscious awareness—consciousness to yield to the higher power of God and embrace the universal differences in another individual and in our world.

All living things need nourishment to grow and survive. The right environment and nutrients make us thrive. In our relationships we must first feed and treat ourselves well so that we can thrive as an individual, then as a partner. This means filling ourselves with enough goodness and God's mercy so we can show compassion toward our partner. A well-known saying often credited to Mahatma Gandhi but paraphrased from another individual says, "Be the change you would like to see in the world." It is our individual actions that cause change. Let us start by changing the single individual *self* within us.

We are the individuals who make up relationships. Changing our relationships begins within the single individual *self*. So, our world of relationships begins to change when we as individuals consciously change. Someone is always watching our individual actions and behaviors for good and bad examples. When our partner sees changes in us, they will be motivated to improve themselves. Together, as a couple, our continual changes transform our relationship.

One of the many songs I learned as a child continues to inspire me as an adult. It is titled, "Oh, Be Careful, Little Eyes," and it leaves the indelible words, "The Father up above is looking down with tender love." The life lesson in the lyrics tells us, "Watch our lips, watch our lips what they say/there is a father up above looking down with tender love/watch our lips, watch our lips what they say." This song continues on with different verses reminding us to be mindful and intentional about our senses. It cautions us to "Watch our eyes what they see/our hearts how they love/our hands what they do/including our feet and where they go."[3]

We communicate not just with our words but also with our energy and actions. We either nurture our marriages and relationships for growth or starve them to death. Emotions are produced from our mental interpretation of what happens. We have to be willing to revise and adjust our mental interpretations to accommodate our partner's perspectives, not just our own views and ideas. We cannot create a new unit of love and emotion and remain stuck in our old ways. We must always be open to learning and expanding our knowledge, be willing to replace old thoughts, and embrace opportunities to improve and grow both as individuals and as partners in our relationships.

Having a sense of curiosity is also important in nurturing relationships. Author and publisher of original positive motivations and inspirational writings called "The Daily Motivator," Ralph Marston Jr. captures the essence of curiosity so beautifully here: "At the heart of curiosity is this love for life and everything in it. The authentically and persistently curious minds are the best informed. Intelligence is more than a measure of what you already know, intelligence is dependent on always being open to learning new things."[4] Curiosity opens our minds to the wealth of knowledge and wisdom of the universal world. Negative emotions such as fear, anger, jealousy, hatred, and vindictiveness close our hearts, minds, and souls to growth.

When we learn to be open and show gratitude for what we already have, we acknowledge abundance in the universe. Focusing on lack invites limiting energies and mindsets into our life. Instead, we must be continuously grateful for who we are and for the partner we are with (if they are desirable in treatment to us and their character). A sense of scarcity invites greed and selfishness. Greed may get us material things, but it will come with a dose of chaos and disharmony in our spirit and ultimately seep into our relationships.

We should generously share our blessings and refill from God's buffet. Psalms 23:1 and 5 say, "The Lord is my Shepherd I shall not want ... He [God] prepares a table before me." God's table is a buffet so we can take what we want as many times as we need to. We just have to open our hearts and minds to acknowledge and accept the invitation to share who we are and what we have.

We are humans with conflicting emotions and energies. Sometimes we struggle to give and share with our partner who may not deserve our good energy. But perpetuating negativity is not conducive to a peaceful and harmonious life. We will always have what we need in spirit through God, even if it is not yet manifested in the physical realm. Let us not become hoarders of the beautiful energies of the universe but instead practice sharing our beautiful energies so goodness and peace will return. Let us allow life, love, and generosity to flow within us and through us with the power of *marrsing*!

THE NEEDS OF OUR RELATIONSHIP

You can have everything in life you want, if you will just help enough other people get what they want.

— Zig Ziglar

We are mediums of flow. Through His universal powers, God gives us the desires of our heart. When we get what we need, want, and ask for, we are supposed to share it with others. We are living in flow when we allow the universe to give us what we need and then pass on energies of love, peace, gratitude, forgiveness, acceptance, and empathy to others. Sharing with others is a positive indicator of embracing life's blessings and rewards. As we grow, we transform into being more content within our spirits and become better versions of ourselves. We are all uniquely created to grow and evolve into more conscious versions of maturity—if we seek wisdom. It is the ebb and flow, give and receive, sow and reap cycles of life that clean our souls and feed our spirits so we can share with our partners. Compassionate sharing nurtures us, allowing us to grow and receive the abundance that replenishes us.

There are many ways we can share our compassion and service with our partners. No matter how much success we achieve, how much money we collect, or how many material possessions we own, we all have basic human needs that only another caring and loving partner can satisfy. Each day we should aim to meet at least one of our partner's human needs.

In her article *Maslow's Hierarchy of Needs Explained*, psychology expert Elizabeth Hopper wrote her contribution on American psychologist Abraham Maslow, who developed "Maslow's Hierarchy of Needs," which posits that we have five basic categories of human need. Sitting in the middle of this five-level hierarchy is the "Love and Belonging" category. Hopper writes, "[this category] involves feeling loved and accepted. This need includes both romantic relationships as well as ties to friends and family members ... Importantly, this need encompasses both feeling loved *and* feeling love towards others."[1] If we are not serving and treating our partner with value, they will seek it from other sources.

Dr. Chapman says, "We give and receive love based on our individual preferences of words of affirmation, receiving gifts, acts of service, physical touch, or quality time."[2] Understanding what is needed to delightfully satisfy our partner's hunger for love is an integral part of having a harmonious and healthy relationship. It requires more than just stating the perfunctory "I love you" and demonstrating the physical acts that heighten emotions to the point of irrational exuberance to create satisfaction.

Bishop Bronner says, "Our life story holds the history of our decisions."[3] Through my experiences, research, and conversations, I have learned that when we say "I love you" it carries different meanings for each of us. The commitment of marriage also carries a different interpretation for each of us. There is a meaningful connection to the nurturing we received during childhood and its manifestation into our adult relationships. This interconnectivity can uncover some unexplored forces that drive each of our individual thoughts, actions, behaviors, and characters. Asking some fundamental questions about our partner provides valuable insight into understanding their dominant influences. We should ask questions such as, "Whose voice and actions shaped their character and views on life and relationships? Who did they respect and trust during their childhood? Who do they admire in adulthood and why?" Understanding the idiosyncrasies of our partners' personalities and becoming consciously aware of their emotional energy sources teaches us how to effectively communicate and share so we grow our relationships and marriages harmoniously.

CHAPTER 20

CAUSES OF DISHARMONY
IN RELATIONSHIPS

You will become what you believe.[1]

— Joel Osteen

What we put out into the world is indicative of what we harbor within us. An angry person holds a lot of anger inside. A kind person holds kindness inside. We generate and exude love if love is inside us. Those who have love within will attract lovers because most people are not attracted to hate, anger, or misery. If we want to maintain loving and committed relationships, we need to stop harboring negative emotions. The low-level emotions of jealousy and anger will always come to visit, but we must not encourage or feed those thoughts and feelings. We can use the *marrsing pause* tool to acknowledge and assess our emotions when we start feeling them. Try to process, reframe, and prepare to release negative thoughts to a higher power. It will be hard at first, but keep trying. When we do, we become more consciously aware of what we choose to allow into our spirit.

The strong emotions within us rule our personality. Emotional contamination causes our feelings and moods created from one situation to creep into another situation. We end up making poor decisions because we do not realize that our feelings toward one situation are carrying over from a previous issue. For example, we feel sure that we are angry about the misplacement of the dinner plates when we remember the way our previous partner also used to misplace them as well.

TRANSGRESSIVE DESIRES AND FORBIDDEN LOVE

We need to balance the dichotomies of realism and
imagination; fun freedom and focused dedication;
traditional and unconventional.[1]

— Brett & Kate McKay

Be open to explore and discover each other's curiosity. It is not acceptable to deny our committed partner and spouse the intimacy they need to satisfy their yearnings and sexual appetites.

Sex is a vital physiological human need for both pleasure and procreation. Whether we believe sex is an essential or non-essential element of active living or not, our personal views about sex do not change the body's natural urge and desire to engage in this beautiful gift of intimate connection between or among the living, breathing entities of the world. Perel says, "The body yearns for sexual indulgence … for most of us, sex and emotions are difficult to untangle."[1] Thoughts and feelings of sex occupy our minds throughout everyday living. Some of us need it daily, some of us want it occasionally, and some of us can enjoy life without engaging in it regularly. However, in each relationship, the topic of sex must be addressed to the satisfaction of each partner. Our committed partner's satisfaction should determine what our sex life entails. This means it should be a mutual understanding about each other's desires and sexual preferences. But if there is sexual satisfaction within the relationship, why would transgressive desires and forbidden love creep in?

From an objective perspective, Perel also posits, "An affair is one story that is experienced by two (or more) people in completely different ways. Hence, it becomes many stories … We need a bridging narrative to help real people navigate the multifaceted experience of infidelity—the motives, the meanings, and the consequences."[2] Those unacknowledged inner worlds of the unexpressed "stories" around transgressive and forbidden behaviors will become weeds and continue to grow out of control in the flower garden of a once promising relationship. Perel also notes, "As tempting as it is to reduce affairs to sex and lies, I prefer to use infidelity as a portal into the complex landscape of relationships and the boundaries we draw to bind them."[3] If left unchecked and not discussed, the weeds of cheating transgressions will choke the nutrients—the love, trust, and caring that the relationship flowers need to thrive.

TEMPTATION LAKE

No temptation has overtaken you except
such as is common to man.

— 1 Corinthians 10:13, NKJV

It's not that some people have willpower, and some don't.
It's that some people are ready to change, and others are not.

— Dr. James Gordon

Temptation is a common experience faced by most committed partners. I refer to the inviting lure of this murky and dangerous assortment of misdeeds and transgressions as "Temptation Lake." Temptation Lake surrounds our homes, workplaces, socialization platforms, and societal interactions.

As committed partners, it is important to create boundaries to protect our relationships and marriages. We must create these boundaries within our thoughts, emotions, and actions to protect the sacredness of our committed relationships. Allen states, "The source and cause of all temptation is in the inward desires; … Outward objects and extraneous powers are utterly powerless to move the soul to sin or to temptation. The outward object is merely the object of the temptation, never the cause. The pure man cannot be tempted, and the wise man cannot be provoked … Self-deprecating fulfillment is the condition of a lusting mind and coveted desires of the heart."[4] When we give in to covetousness outside our committed relationships and marriages, we act against the vows we made to our partners. We seek alternate desires that will destroy the trust we have created within our relationships.

Temptation Lake is full of eager fish of infidelity, adultery, cheating, lying, and deception. For some, it constantly invites us to jump in for a quick swim. But if we give in to the temptation and the anticipated thrill of getting wet for a short dip, we will be swallowed up below the sinkhole of continuing destructive behaviors. Cloud and Townsend notes, "A marriage is only as strong as what it costs to protect it. In other words, you value what you invest in. If you have spent time, effort, and sacrifice preserving your [relationship or] marriage from other influences, your odds of a solid [relationship or] marriage are better ... Those who value the preciousness of their marriage will pay a high price to preserve it ... This is why wedding vows often include the phrase "forsaking all others."[5] How strong is your commitment to your partner? Can it withstand the many temptations lurking outside the walls of your relationship?

By giving in to temptation, we risk losing what we have built because of one euphoric moment. Is it worth it? Is giving in to temptation worth the ensuing marital and emotional turmoil that will most likely result from that momentary transgression?

Each time we are tempted, we can take a *marrsing pause* and do a quick cost-benefit analysis to think deeper about the aftereffects of what that little jump into Temptation Lake will cost. If we settle for a one-time swim, we lose access to our partner's prestigious private beach, the excitement of riding the waves of a passion-filled relationship, and the prosperity of growing a trusting partnership and family. In his book *The Strangest Secret*, Earl Nightingale says, "Our goal is in the future, it is not about getting the things we want now in life."[6] That means we should always be aspiring and working toward something greater, not losing what we have been working toward for momentary escapades.

In one of his televised sermons, Bishop Bronner preaches, "Wisdom is realizing that there are future consequences of our current decisions. Our decisions determine our conduct, our character, and our destiny."[7] A *marrsing pause* can bring our thoughts into rationalization mode so we can ask ourselves, "Will our actions help or harm our relationship and marriage goals?" Bronner further cautions us, "Never sacrifice the ultimate on the immediate."[8] Remember the laws of God and that the universe is always at work in all that we do.

A. R. Bernard, pastor of the Christian Cultural Center Megachurch in Brooklyn, New York said it well during his *Super Soul Sunday* appearance on the OWN network. He remarked that, "Love is the ability to give of ourselves without expecting anything in return. But lust is the desire to satisfy only the individual self."[9] Lust is instant gratification with long lasting consequences.

CHARACTER AND INFLUENCES

Let a man radically alter his thoughts, and
he will be astonished at the rapid transformation
it will affect in the material conditions of his life.

— James Allen, *As A Man Thinketh*

We should marry a person because of their heart, spirit, and character, not just for their facial features. The personality blueprint that unveils the true inner partner lies below the outward personality, charm, and ego. There are so many aspects to who we are as a person. From a relationship perspective, the emotional and psychological aspects of our character determine how we engage in love, why we love, and how we demonstrate our love.

Through the ebb and flow of our relationships, we learn that silent suffering is not patience. If someone keeps knowingly harming us but continues those actions to satisfy their personal desires, then they are abusing us. Selfishness stifles relationships. Abuse kills relationships. Relationships are about serving others, not selfishly using or abusing our partners. As the movie title *Get Out* implies, leave before you are ruined. It is simply not good for any human being to continually allow another person to destroy them. Sometimes the habitual taker will be so charming while they are hurting us, that we get swept into their manipulative embrace thinking they care about us. The abuser will do one good act after ten bad ones and expect us to focus only on the one good behavior and never mention the ten bad incidents. Be careful! It is only a deterrent to appease us and keep up their manipulative embrace.

These personality types will tease with one good behavior as a means of inserting glimmers of hope to keep their partner hanging on. They will repeatedly promise to do better in due time, but they will just use the time to seek another unsuspecting partner who will ultimately become another victim of their charm and deception. The tools of these manipulators' trade are generally charm, secrecy, and control. They are skilled at using these tools to continue their relationship until they decide to move on to the next victim.

Manipulators are always actively looking for other mates who fit their general criteria of subservience and desperation. They target emotionally unfulfilled individuals who are obsessively looking for *anyone* to be with.

Be careful, do not become a victim of the ever-widening categories of psychological personality disorders. If we are SAD (single, available, and desperate), we will be easy prey. Manipulators are skillful, smooth talkers who know the right words to say to get what they want. They understand their target's desperation and are skilled at doing the impressive deeds that will have us feeling like we have found a knight in shining armor. We must be careful about what the armor is covering up. The armor stays on long enough to highlight sparkles of good until they can take all they need before we realize we are being victimized.

Partners with good, genuine character will build and gain more trust and value throughout the relationship as they grow together. Bishop Bronner imparts, "If we don't have good character, we can't have good influence, and we'll lose respect if others don't trust us … Don't be a private failure and a public success."[1] One aim of the *marrsing* mission is for partners to grow trust and achieve harmony in their relationships and homes. There is a song titled "You Can Tell a Lot About a Man" by Terry and Barbi Franklin that goes, "You can tell a lot about a man by the way he treats his wife/Does he make his home a haven or is it filled with fear and strife?"[2] Are our words and actions toward our partners creating love or fear in our homes? Are our words causing harmony or strife? If negative seeds of anger, fear, violence, and vengeance are always being deposited in our relationship and marriages, do we stay together, seek help, or end the relationship?

In his book *Lead the Field*, Nightingale says, "The reasonable man has integrity, he's honest and truthful. Who we are speaks so much louder than what we say."[3] Our repeated behavior defines our character. Socrates (credited to Plato) commented, "An unexamined life is not worth living."[4] Let us take the time to begin examining our lives, starting with the *marrsing DIG*. Then we can take action to be valuable and worthy partners!

CHAPTER 21

DISEMPOWERING RELATIONSHIPS

Whenever we are in a transition,
God is getting ready to take us to a new place.[1]

— Bishop Dale C. Bronner

Relationships are about serving each other, but sometimes it's better to be alone than to be in a bad relationship. Licensed therapist Michelle Overman notes, "Persistent passive-aggressive behavior can be toxic and result in an unhealthy dynamic; we should feel empowered to walk away from harmful relationships."[1] Growth comes with change and maturity. As we grow in age, knowledge, and wisdom, we become more conscious of our perspectives on life. As partners, we can engineer our growth as a harmonious union of two or as a divisiveness of ones. Communal growth encourages trust and harmony, while individualistic growth spurns selfishness and animosity. Couples are not supposed to compete against each other; our goals should align. Competition, lack of support, and selfish endeavors starve a relationship of its strength and unity. Our vibrational aura and individual energies can collide and dissipate if both partners are not consciously working toward a mutual destiny.

Broken vows will invite negative emotions and void our commitments. The vow of "'til death do us part" does not specify the death of *what*. The emotional turmoil of two human beings coexisting in a negative environment as one unit is detrimental to staying true to those words if physical death is imminent because of strife. When vows disintegrate, they damage love connections and dissolve relational connections.

Too much anger and vengeance can kill security and affection. The end of a committed marital journey may occur while we are still physically alive and have lingering love. For some marital journeys, rather than the physical death of the body, it is the death of trust, sex, or intimacy, or the death of the authentic love between partners, which will cause our commitment to dissipate.

Leaving a long-term relationship is a life-altering decision, but it releases the disempowering restraints that choke the positive energies needed to flourish in life. It clears the space for our minds to embark on a more loving, spiritual, and peaceful path. It is not circumstances that determine how our life will unfold; it is making the choice to stop allowing someone else to disempower us with different forms of hurtful behaviors, then expecting obedience to their fury and demands. American psychologist J. Martin Kohe, author of *Your Greatest Power*, reminds us that, "The greatest gift that a person possesses is the power to choose."[2] Saying, "I didn't have a choice" is not an acceptable excuse for enduring an unhealthy relationship. We must not relinquish our fundamental and inalienable human right to choose the best environment, most healthy environment, and Godly options for us. Choosing to walk away for our life, health, and safety is exercising our power to protect ourselves.

Abuse is when someone intentionally and repeatedly hurts us. It comes in many forms, such as verbal and physical. Verbal abuse is when someone uses disrespectful words and tones when they talk to us. One example I personally detest is calling a female the derogatory word "bitch." Examples of emotional abuse are constantly cheating and having multiple affairs of infidelity. Violent and harmful contact is physical abuse. Being manipulative and controlling is another form of abuse. All forms of abuse are damaging, disempowering, and destructive to both the person and the relationship. Raising our conscious awareness to understand what we need in our relationships will help us recognize behavior patterns that are harmful to our well-being and our relationships.

There is a popular phrase that says, "Love is blind." But eventually, the blinders start getting tighter and squeeze the life out of the relationship and the individual. A reality check on a regular basis can provide eye-opening revelations that are being hidden by our idealistic aspirations. Taking the blinders off "every once in a while" means tapping into our conscious awareness of how our relationship is aligning with its purpose. We can start with questions like, "Is my current relationship adding to or depleting my worth?" We must value ourselves enough to walk away from people, situations, and relationships that are hurting, depleting, and destroying us.

CHAPTER 22

EMOTIONAL ENTANGLEMENTS AND COLLISIONS—PSYCHE AND PERSONALITY

When we begin to find the relationship difficult to retain,
we will find that we need to invest an exhausting amount
of time and resources in maintaining it.

— Napoleon Hill

The reality is I was suffering, everything looked great
on the outside, but I was crying myself to sleep at night.
Marriage is a place where you shouldn't need protection.
It should be the place where you can be your most vulnerable.

— Sarah Jakes

In our fury, we should never unload our trauma-infused frustrations on our partners, spouses, or friends. We may apologize afterward, but the damage cannot be undone. Once we inflict an emotional wound, it never heals; it fades into our memory. It may not hurt as much after an apology, but it always leaves a scar on our emotional well-being. Most of the time, our frustrations with others are all about what we perceive or what we assume in our minds. The meanings that we put on someone else's actions are our own internal interpretations of an external event. We do not always know what the other person is going through or what they are feeling. We do not know what experience in their past may translate the circumstances into a totally different and traumatizing event for them.

I cannot complete this book without mentioning three of the psychologically impaired personalities that are easily misconceived and prevalent throughout society and relationships: The narcissist, sociopath, and psychopath. In the beginning of relationships, a narcissist, sociopath, or psychopath will charm their way and smoothly gain power over docile and unsuspecting individuals without raising suspicion about their conniving objectives.

Recognizing these personality types is critical for understanding psychological manipulation. When we are psychologically ignorant, we lose ourselves in the pits of manipulation, control, and abuse. Our hopefulness for better outcomes convinces us to stay in a relationship even when the path shows signs of danger. Becoming a more consciously aware partner requires changing our thought processes and adjusting the lens we use to see our part-ners' behaviors and idiosyncrasies.

When partners in a committed relationship routinely lie, cheat, and deceive, they are showing who they truly are inside. One of the most com-mon tactics of narcissists, sociopaths, and psychopaths is gaslighting. Licensed clinical psychologist and professor of psychology at California State Univer-sity in Los Angeles, Dr. Ramani Durvasula, says, "If you've ever felt the need to record a conversation to play it back to that person as proof or so you can be sure you heard it right, you're being gaslighted."[1] Sometimes a partner who is truly remorseful for these behaviors on a one-time basis can be forgiven on the first occurrence if they are genuinely sorry for their actions and make efforts to change themselves. But whenever these behaviors are symptoms of underlying psychological, pathological, or mental disorders, then we should seriously ask for spiritual guidance to protect our hearts and sanity, if we choose to stay in a relationship with them.

Narcissists, sociopaths, and psychopaths are great charmers and sweet talkers. They permeate the fabric of personal and intimate connections with their smooth-talking, controlling, domineering, manipulative, and self-ab-sorbed personalities. They wittingly charm their way into our lives, hearts, and souls with such grace and charisma that we get swept off our feet and taken for exciting and romantic rides on their personal "manipulation-ship." They crave control and demand subservience from their partners under the term "loyalty." They only care about their own needs and feelings, and see their partners as a resource for their supply and boosters of their overinflated ego. Whenever we start asking questions, disagreeing, or challenging their behaviors, we will become victims of their egos. Until we become consciously aware of their misaligned behaviors, we will be blinded by their innate ability to mimic caring emotions.

In reality, narcissists, sociopaths, and psychopaths are usually deeply inse-cure people attempting to hide their true feelings about themselves. To manage their painful emotions, they will sometimes retaliate with passive-aggressive behaviors while inflating their ego. They idolize themselves and act entitled toward things and opportunities in life because they are incapable of empa-thy. Most have experienced dysfunctional relationships in which they felt rejected, often by their parents or close guardians. Licensed marriage and family therapist Michelle Overman, writes, "Rejected individuals feel less empathy for others and are consequently less willing to cooperate with and help their partners whenever they feel rejected."[2] She also notes, "After being rejected, individuals are especially likely to lash out against the rejecter and to aggress against their innocent partners."[3] Disharmony grows and multiplies in relationships because of the dominant characteristics of these personality types: deception, lack of empathy, self-service, and pathological lying. Attachment theories and numerous studies on the connection between psychopaths and their lack of empathy demonstrate that these disorders stem from either not being loved or their childhood traumas.

Choosing to maintain a sane relationship with any of these three personality types means we constantly exist as subservient partners who provide them with their resources. This requires being someone who they can manipulate and control—someone who loyally obeys their instructions and requests. Personalities like this keep partners who conform to their quests for attention and constant commendation. Overman advises us to "be open to their feelings: Their behavior might come from their own hurt or insecurity. Take responsibility for any part of the perceived issue that is appropriate."[4] However, the longer we endure the effects of psychopathic behaviors, sociopathic tendencies, and pathological lying, the more damaged we become.

Smith contributes her expert advice on addressing the intense anger these people might display: "Those who come off as aggressive towards others may use anger and rage as a smokescreen for their true feelings and emotions. Their 'intense anger' is usually a result of not being in touch with their feelings, or they may not want to explore or address their feelings. So they use anger as a way to cover them up."[5] Allowing the harshness of negative behaviors to persist in our lives will gradually deplete us. So when we are being constantly mistreated, exiting the relationship might be the safest option.

Narcissists, sociopaths, and psychopaths tend to be love paupers according to the myriad of research on these personalities. They are love-poor because they lack empathy. They cannot truly love you back because of their inability to feel or experience sincere care or positive emotions for others. They will gravitate toward others who will "do" for them and stroke their egos. If you do not satisfy their demands for their self-elevation, they will jettison you from their (relation)ship and move on.

For us to change behaviors, we require a strong motivational reason to either achieve or avoid something in our life or relationship. But before we get motivated, we have to become aware of the challenge that's affecting us or decide on a goal to aspire towards. Otherwise, only temporary adjustments will happen. In a conversation I had with one of my goddaughters, she profoundly remarked that, "People don't change, they modify their behavior to fit their needs, wants, and desires for their current situations." Coming from a much younger "millennial mind" I found this quite insightful and an intriguing argument to research.

Can sociopaths and narcissists be rehabilitated to become conscientious partners? I curiously ask, can individuals with psychological challenges control their thoughts and vengeful desires enough to have long-term harmonious relationships?

Therapy has proven beneficial in improving many psychological and mental personality disorders and challenges. For these partners, help is available if they truly want to change. But they must first acknowledge their impact on the relationship and have the desire to improve themselves. I believe people who are genuine in their intentions and want to have authentic relationships can make conscious efforts toward transforming their thoughts and actions. Tackling dominant characteristics is challenging, but betterment comes through ongoing, intentional efforts. Incorporating *marrsing* tools into their relational connections will be a conscientious decision towards improving relationship behaviors.

Ultimately, each partner in a relationship must decide what the purpose of the relationship is and how much they are willing to sacrifice for the life they want together. Staying with a partner should offer more than relief from the "uncommitted single person" status. The wealth and value of a relationship should be a fulfilling partnership, not a depleting one.

Marrsing Thought

Don't 'fall' in love if you are the only one falling. Falling alone hurts and it gives the other person opportunity to step on or over you.

Angella Watkis Francis

CHAPTER 23

MANAGING OUR CHANGE

If you get the inside right,
the outside will fall into place.[1]

— Eckhart Tolle

You can't change how people treat you or
what they say about you. All we can do is change
the way we react to it.

— Mahatma Gandhi

Change is a process that takes time and effort. Transforming ourselves, our relationships, and our marriages requires consistent effort. Just as emerging life is a cycle of egg meeting sperm, to the growth of a fetus, and finally to birth, we have to keep persevering through the metamorphic stages in the difficult times. Ecclesiastes 7:14 says, "In the day of prosperity be joyful, but in the day of adversity consider: Surely God has appointed the one as well as the other, so that man can find out nothing will come after him." This means both the challenges and the opportunities are all part of God's transformational work in our lives.

Transformation does not just happen, it requires fresh intentions, higher awareness, and consistent action. One of my favorite singers is Jamaican reggae icon Bob Marley. In his lyrics of "Redemption Song" he commands us to, "Emancipate yourselves from mental slavery."[1] It is only the individual *self* that has the power from within to get rid of self-doubt, anger, shame, jealousy, vengeance, and any negative thoughts that occupy our minds and end up ruling our beliefs and actions. Negative thoughts tend to multiply quickly and lead to destructive behaviors. When we engage in self-defeating actions and behaviors, it means we have allowed the caravan of negative thoughts to run freely along the tracks of our minds.

We are on this earth to live fully! Allow the energies of the universe to flow through us while we are sharing in the earth's abundance. This requires consistent work on clearing the personal blocks that are preventing us from fully enjoying the wealth of the universe. Music is one way to keep ourselves in flow. From the lyrics of Marley's song "Trenchtown Rock" he encouragingly says, "One good thing about music, when it hits you feel no pain/so hit me with music."[2] Multi-award-winning independent documentary director and writer, Elena Mannes, supported these lyrics on a scientific and cultural perspective with data to corroborate the value of music on our spirit and soul in her book and PBS documentary *The Music Instinct: Science and Song.* She states, "*Science and Song* provided a ground-breaking exploration into how and why the human organism—and the whole ebb and flow of the cosmos— is moved by the undeniable effect of music.[3] Mannes further shares, "We instinctively understand the vibrational frequency of music. It's the universal language that transcends race, gender, culture, and religion. ... Sound is a healing component." I believe we should indulge in music regularly. Maya Angelou, internationally acclaimed American poet, storyteller, activist, and autobiographer, also supports the power of music with her famous quote, "There is a spirit in all music, the spirit has the ability to conjure up thoughts, even pictures of something that happened, or you wished would happen, or you anticipate happening."[4] As the lyrics we listen to manifest in our spirit, they can ignite our creative flow of ideas for our relationships.

We must be careful what we invite into our spirit. The lyrics and sounds we allow in can create good or bad thoughts within our minds. Listening to songs from the days of our innocent youth can bring back deep nostalgic feelings that once brought us free-flowing joy and positive energy—the kind of music that used to rule our childhood hearts and open our souls to the vast kingdom of exciting imaginations.

The brain can only think about one thing at a time. We can use the power of *marrsing* to activate the conscious mind and interrupt the train of destructive thoughts carousing along in our minds that can derail our aspirational missions. Repeating or chanting *marrsing* practices to a favorite rhythm, rhyme, or affirmation can trigger our inner vibe and invoke God's guidance in our decisions. The additional tools, *marrsing breath* and *marrsing pause*, are effective in switching our thought processes and activating our creative visualization toward our higher conscious intentions and more positive outcomes. Taking a *marrsing breath*, say "marr" on the inhale and "sing" on the exhale.

Likewise, memorizing affirmative scriptures and positive motivational words enriches, supports, and strengthens us as we raise ourselves upward in this world. Gaining extraordinary wisdom from God's words empowers us to live abundantly with intentionality, love unconditionally, and share more generously. We need to develop a sacred connection with God's words and let the scriptures guide us to becoming Godly inspired partners and spouses. As a part of uncovering and acknowledging who we are as individuals deep within ourselves, we have to allow our souls and spirits to be guided by a force that is omnipresent and more powerful than ourselves. Whether it is through prayer, meditation, or devotion, we can choose and memorize scriptures that speak to our spirituality and our individual life journey. Keeping motivational and inspiring quotes and verses inscribed on our hearts and in our memories will strengthen our power and grow our faith so we can become enlightened about God's guidance, protection, and plan for our lives.

No one can give us success. Success is an achievement. We achieve success by investing time, energy, and resources toward our goals. *Marrsing* is about achieving higher conscious awareness toward our intentioned relationships. It is embarking on a mission to reach success within ourselves and our relationships with our partners and spouses. To achieve success, we have to invest in the *marrsing* tools.

Investing time and effort in *marrsing* resources changes our thoughts, actions, and behaviors. We can choose to live intentionally, love consciously, and share compassionately. By acknowledging our purpose, power, and passion, we can change ourselves and enhance our thoughts and actions toward transforming our relationships. In his book *The Power of Now*, Tolle famously says, "Don't spend too much time trying to manage the outside. If we get inside right, the outside will fall into place. Everything that matters happens on the inside of us."[5] It all starts with our thinking.

Life is a series of breakthroughs into the next phases, stages, and levels. Our blessings of today can become the sources of our disappointments and heartaches later in life. The people, things, and places we yearn for now can become our problems and regrets later. Learn to expect and survive the breakthroughs and the breakdowns. However, we should also know when to move on. Staying in a disharmonious relationship can stifle our aspirations. If the relationship no longer has a definite purpose to improve and strive toward, we should analyze our options and decide accordingly. Partnerships need a purpose. If our intuition guides us toward another purpose, communicate with each other and make a choice. If we believe in our choices and own the consequences and outcomes, we will find peace and harmony on a different journey.

God works through us when we are weak, broken, and tired. Faith is a powerful antidote to carry within us for strength. Whatever challenges we are facing, whenever we think we cannot survive, we just have to stay focused on our goals and reaffirm our belief that God and the universe will bring us through. The scripture in Philippians 4:13 tells us, "I can do all things through Him who gives me strength." We build and get stronger through the rebuilding of our life muscles. Belief will take care of fifty percent of getting us to where we need to be, not only physically, but also mentally, psychologically, and emotionally.

Embarking on this new path of a *marrsing* mission is an antidote for enhancing and transforming our relationships psychologically, emotionally, and mentally. We achieve this by aligning the purpose of our thoughts and actions with the level of harmony, respect, and appreciation we want in our relationships. Believing in the power we have within us as individuals and partners puts us at the starting line.

Being able to give of ourselves and our possessions means that we are actively living, using, and sharing the energies of the universe. Love remains one of the most powerful and abundant energies, and it transcends within the universe. Love should not be a transactional commodity. If we are constantly demanding an immediate return for the emotions and attention that we share with our partners, then we are conducting a transaction of lust to satisfy our own individual needs. Like using a bank to cash a check, withdrawing our deposits as soon as we make them, and not allowing our deposits to grow and multiply, demanding an immediate return on love diminishes the value within our relationships.

We must take care of our minds, thoughts, and feelings and allow them to heal from any previous traumas or negative experiences. When two healthy hearts come together, they create energies of wellness and passion.

Emotionally healthy and thriving hearts are more energized to enjoy each other through unrepressed sexual freedom and the curiosity to try anything with an adventurous spirit. Adventures within our relationships excite, nourish, and grow our connection.

We must also address and repair the impact of any negative past experiences, so we can free our hearts and minds to enjoy more fulfilling sex and life experiences. Our inhibitions and insecurities develop from childhood experiences. Past traumatic situations can impede our sexual fulfillment and joy, ultimately affecting and damaging our spirit of intimacy, romantic curiosity, and the overall health and happiness of our sexual expressions in our relationships. Addressing them gives us the freedom to indulge in the goodness of our relationships and the excitement of enjoying each other.

We have to be consciously aware of the emotional, mental, and psychological dichotomies performing their juggling acts between the minds of the *self* and the committed partner when we collide. We can avoid perpetuating a war of words if we take a pause, breathe, then consciously formulate our responses. A *marrsing pause* gives us a time-out to intentionally focus on how we act out toward our partners and avoid re-acting to the situation. Doing a quick *marrsing pause* before verbalizing our thoughts and reacting negatively prevents verbal wounds and emotional scars. This can be challenging, especially when negative emotions start roaring in with their companions of anger and vengeance. But we must consciously pause to positively reframe the raging thoughts.

Trusting God to take care of our insecurities, temptations, and negative emotions of anger, greed, jealousy, vengeance, and hatred will lighten our spirits. Psalms 55:22 says, "Cast your cares on the Lord, and He will sustain you." This means we can release these negative emotions to the Lord through prayer and meditation. During the *marrsing pause*, we can visualize ourselves literally handing them over to God. This is the time when we will denounce our human *selves* and invoke God's power to guide us while we are sorting through our emotions.

As responsible individuals in relationships, we are adults who yearn for positive communications and caring interactions. We can achieve this by consciously avoiding angry outbursts and physical altercations to solve misunderstandings or disagreements. We must take care of the people we love, not hurt them.

Marrsing Thought

Could we be profoundly mistaking the disappointments along our life journey as our final destiny rather than a re-direction onto a more progressive path?

Angella Watkis Francis

CHAPTER 24

PRESERVING OUR RELATIONSHIPS AND ENVIRONMENT

The human behavior flows from three main sources:
desire, emotion and knowledge.

— Plato

Self-control, which is essential, is like a muscle—
the more you exercise it, the stronger it gets.[1]

— Bridget Grenville-Cleave

Relationships are one of the most important things in life—not money, success, or promotions. I had the profound experience of sitting with my dying sister. Most of us will not realize how death and Near-Death Experiences (NDEs) teach us how to live until we are faced with a life-altering situation. She had achieved her aspirations of significant financial, professional, and personal success during her lifetime. At the most critical moment in her life when she most needed compassionate support, none of the money, properties, or corporate titles could offer her comfort. The people who she had valuable relationships with were the ones who provided care and comfort when she needed it most. My sister's death taught me the valuable lesson that we get our lasting needs from our healthy and harmonious relationships and not from financial and material gains.

We cannot put off living, loving, and sharing with the people who mean the most to us in life. If we knew we would die tomorrow, would we want our partners there to comfort us as we transition? If the answer is yes, then it is important to treat our partners with appreciation and respect. We must not let the last sacred moments of life be ones of regrets and apologies. They should be about sanctifying good memories.

As we embark on our new *marrsing* journey, managing and preserving our energy and emotions will start to become a priority in our daily lives. We will become more conscious about the energies we allow to rule our spirits. As we evolve into better versions of ourselves, we will begin exercising our power to bring awareness to our thoughts, actions, language, and behavior.

Over time, our anxiety-filled life of contentious responses and mean-spirited selfishness in our relationships will be transformed into spirit-driven unions and partnerships of intentional service. We will raise our levels of consciousness to the point where we begin to measure the time and energy it costs us to engage in negative situations and confrontations, resulting in an elevated level of awareness within our thoughts, feelings, and behaviors. We will choose to use our valuable energy for planting seeds of goodness and service rather than resentment or retaliation, and we will sow seeds of hope rather than confusion. And we will begin directing our energy toward cultivating seeds of compassion rather than weeds of revenge.

Harmonious relationships help us become spiritually healthy because of the positive energy and vibes that we generate when we are happy, trusting, caring, kind, and intentionally good in our interactions with our partners. Synergistic relationships generate high energies of fulfillment and satisfaction that make our environment, relationships, and marriages harmonious. Harmony within our homes and relationships generates happiness in our lives and hearts. We must all get on the *marrsing* path of living intentionally, loving consciously, and sharing generously!

Marrsing Thought

If Love is the reason we got married,
'til death' means we can part after the love dies.
Not when the physical life ends.

Angella Watkis Francis

MARRSING CLAUSE

Being able to assess reality with completely clear eyes,
while simultaneously exercising the capacity to
see it romantically, is a rare, but an attainable gift.
The contact between our different beliefs/ideas/interests
creates an access mission to new knowledge and planes
of existence that wouldn't have been possible otherwise.

— Winston Churchill

The journey of our marriages and relationships will include many revisions throughout the years to accommodate the different stages of life. Anticipating these stages in the beginning and throughout our relationships supports the *marrsing* mission.

We need to capture our initial aspirations about our marital partnerships as mutual agreements and reminders of the reasons we committed to one another. Our expectations and desires about how our lives will unfold throughout these relationships might not reflect how they will actually play out. But we can capture them with a *marrsing clause*.

A *marrsing clause* helps us as partners to explore the intricate details of our relationships and set our intentions for the DNA and relational outcomes of our marriages. This includes having discussions to address any relationship deviations from the *marrsing clause* commitments, allowing room for intervention. When all the trust, love, motivation, respect, appreciation, and effort of reconciliation have failed, we can amicably chart our next phase. If we create and include a separation clause from the onset, we can freely choose to end the relationship without engaging in hurtful arguments and contentious actions.

Partners in committed relationships must share more than intimacy—the same roof, mortgage, rent, children, and bills. Drafting a *marrsing clause* is an important first step in beginning the mutual mission of living a *marrsing* life together.

The marriage journey begins after wedding festivities end. Let the *marrsing clause* be the guide for our married life. While speaking during her breakout session at the 2019 Bay Path University's 24th Annual Women's Leadership Conference, business consultant, *New York Times* bestselling author, and global thought leader Cy Wakeman states, "Inertia is detrimental to progress."[1] Talking about succeeding in work and life she says, "Growth comes in small stages, so we have to keep moving and learning so we can continue to renew for change." Understanding the aspects of living together, discovering intimate details about each other, and getting to know about each other's idiosyncrasies happens in stages and sometimes brings some level of frustration as we progress in our relationships. However, the development phase of our commitments can be made much easier with a *marrsing clause*. The *marrsing clause* is a mutual agreement that outlines what we will do for, to, and with each other for the benefit of reaching our life goals and having harmonious relationships together. We must work together as a partnership unit as partners who care about each other and the success of our relationships.

American former First Lady and activist Eleanor Roosevelt, one of the world's most admired women, said in her initial statement, "it was not a question of what one believed … but how one lived one's beliefs." These words have been modernized into: "One's philosophy is not best expressed in words; it is expressed in the choices one makes … and the choices we make are ultimately our responsibility."[2] Choosing to have a *marrsing clause* as part of our commitment to each other demonstrates our devotion to the success of our relationships. It is a choice to create our own personally designed commitment blueprint as a positive indication that we are dedicated to being intentional about having a successful relationship. This will be our preparation for success rather than battling raw emotions and eventual failure. The *clause* helps us as partners to live out our uniquely drafted set of "I do's" translated into "we will" statements.

The *marrsing clause* defines what our commitment means to each other. It will outline our purposeful direction and our intentions to do the following:

- **Indemnify our relationship** – around each other's values, needs, desires, and expectations
- **Declare the terms and boundaries** of our relationship

❈ **Outline the purpose** of our mutual goals and aspirations within our relationship

Our "we will" agreement *clause* will change as our relationships evolve. Depending on the age, stage, and phase that we are living through, the intensity of our purpose, power, and passion will reflect our intentions, consciousness, and service as we grow and mature together. Bishop Bronner says, "The quality of our decisions will depend on our maturity."[3] He further cautions us by saying, "Maturity doesn't necessarily come with age. It comes with the application of our knowledge, through wisdom and understanding." Individuals who adapt the *marrsing* concept and join the life mission to live, love, and share with the power of *marrsing* are clearly signaling maturity. Joining the *marrsing* mission demonstrates that we are being responsible for the thoughts, actions, and behaviors that we put into our relationships and the universe.

Our relationships will be emotionally harmonious if we create a *marrsing clause* to guide us in how we share, nurture, and protect our emotions. It will create a para*DIG*m shift in how we engage in our relationships and ultimately redefine the authenticity of our intimacy. The clause will encourage us to start rethinking and reassessing the way we share our intimate energy and emotions. We should not *give away* our love because we will end up empty when someone takes it and leaves. We should not *fall* in love either because falling hurts. Instead, we should *share* our love and seek emotional harmony for the stage, age, and time of life that we are experiencing. Each phase of our lives requires specific emotional needs and partnership support.

Bishop Bronner preaches that the quality of our choices depend on specific traits:

❈ **Spirituality:** Sensitivity and acknowledgment of a higher power, a holy and ever-present spirit.
❈ **Emotional State:** We must heal before making decisions. We usually make poor decisions when we are desperate. Emotional volatility (desperation) will lead to bad decisions.
❈ **Physical Condition:** Being hungry, tired, sleepy, or sick impacts our ability to make rational decisions.

❂ **Moral Values:** Our principles and moral judgments measure our behaviors and influence the quality of our decisions.

❂ **Tradition/Culture:** These can blind us. Our eyes cannot see what the mind is not prepared to comprehend. The mind does not have eyes so it cannot see how the world order has changed. Therefore, we have to be willing to adjust our cultural beliefs.[4]

We can use the *marrsing clause* to help us identify and understand our possible weaknesses that can easily derail us. The *marrsing clause* guides us as individuals and couples in developing our resistance to destructive enticements. We get to design our own set of goals toward the purpose we are committing to in our marriages. We can include safeguards in our *clause* to keep us from wandering into the muddy waters of temptation, which will help us avoid becoming a victim of the mass infestation lurking beneath.

CHAPTER 26

MARRSING ON
THE BRAIN—A JOURNEY
OF SUCCESS

*Deliberate Conscious Evolution—Means we can change
the neuropathy of our brains to change our habits.*

— John Assaraf

*A person with a growth mindset believes that
he or she can get smarter, better, or more skilled at
something through sustained effort—which is
exactly what neuroplasticity tells us."*

— Courtney E. Ackerman,
What is Neuroplasticity? A Psychologist Explains

*M*arrsing thought energy can change the chemical arrangement in our brain by interrupting brain waves with thoughts about the purpose, power, and passion of our *marrsing* mission. When we take a *marrsing pause*, we get to rearrange our thoughts, words, and actions by repeating the word *marrsing* rather than saying sharp, destructive words out loud while we contemplate positive responses. Hill reminds us that "mastery over our tongue is important."[2]

Our brains are our "computers," and our habits are the software that runs the machinery of our brains. Our thoughts tweak the machine. One of the leading behavioral and mindset experts in the world, John Assaraf, says there are three parts to our habits:

- **Emotional:** something triggers us to evoke a specific emotion
- **Behavioral:** our response (action) to the emotional trigger
- **Neurological/biological:** the reward results from our response and action; what we hoped to achieve or receive[3]

The brain is our body's translation tool and *marrsing* is a type of automaticity. In their article "Neural Bases of Automaticity," authors Mathieu Servant of University of Franche-Comté, Peter Cassey of Vanderbilt University, and Geoffrey F. Woodman of Vanderbilt University state that, "automaticity allows us to perform tasks in a fast, efficient, and effortless manner after sufficient practice."[4] By using it to consistently practice pausing to breathe each time we are about to react to our partners, *marrsing* makes for an easy go-to tool in our relationship communications. As our brain shifts through the repetitions of the *marrsing breath* and pause, it activates the prefrontal cortex portion of the brain that is responsible for logical thinking and helps us to choose rational conscious-loving responses.

Scientific research tells us that the association to a bad past is triggered when a similar thought or scenario takes place. When these memories are activated, they evoke fear in our minds and we either fight, freeze, or run away. To calm ourselves, the brain needs to switch. When we feel anxious, fearful, or angry, the *marrsing breath* pause can be used to make that switch. Taking deep, intentional breaths switches your brain from the state of fight or flight to a calmer setting where you can become logical in your thinking and make rational decisions that will preserve your relationships rather than damage them.

Negative thinking is a major contributor to mental health issues. Individuals who have experienced trauma and dysfunction without receiving healing tend to have difficulty redirecting and processing their negative emotions. Using a simple, readily available switch exercise like the *marrsing pause* or *marrsing breath* to initiate the switch begins the process of changing negative thought patterns into positive, productive thoughts. When we do this, we show monumental improvement in our emotional states and our behaviors.

Below is a quick *marrsing* exercise:

1. **Acknowledge:** Become aware of our thoughts and the immediate emotions that they evoke.
2. **Breathe:** Through mindful breathing, release emotions (waves of energy) and clear our thoughts.
3. **Pause:** Take a moment to understand the situation from different perspectives; we do not need to react immediately to what is being acknowledged.
4. **Align:** Think through the possible outcomes; Will our response help or hurt the relationship? Is our response going to be constructive or destructive to our relationship or marriage?

Our thoughts influence our relationships, lives, and environments. Everything we experience gets translated as "good" or "bad" based on our own thoughts and interpretations. We have the power to change what does not align with our aspirations, objectives, and overall purpose of our relationships and lives. By restructuring our thought processes from destructive to constructive, we can reframe our thoughts about a person or situation by changing the meaning from within our minds. For example, if two spouses cheat on each other, the outcome will probably be different based on the thoughts, actions, and circumstances of each partner and their goals and purpose of their respective relationships.

By thinking and behaving with intentionality about our relationships, we become better versions of ourselves and evolve into more conscious partners. The power of *marrsing* helps us use our spiritual and logical thinking skills to stop the negative pattern of destructive thoughts and actions that can cloud our judgment. If we use the simple but powerful process of *marrsing* to intentionally raise our consciousness and acknowledge, breathe, pause, and align our thoughts, we can better manage negative and stress-inducing relationship situations. We can begin transforming our behaviors for the betterment of our individual selves and our relationships. When we improve who we are as individuals, we live with intentionality and peace in our hearts. That internal calm and peace can effectively align our actions with the goals we want to achieve.

Change begins with a thought and takes time. We can begin by thinking and saying the word *marrsing* each time we start a thought pertaining to our relationships. We then ask ourselves, does this thought or action align with who we want to be as a partner or person? With a *marrsing breath*, we can review and analyze impending thoughts or actions. Positive thoughts, actions, and behaviors enhance and improve our relationships. In his blog post titled "Universal Law: Repeat What You Want and You Will Get It," Kaihan Krippendorff says, "Keep singing the same note and the universe's echo will eventually build it into a perfectly tuned symphony."[5] When we emancipate our mind and free ourselves of negative thinking that creates relationship roadblocks, we begin to elevate our consciousness and create peace and harmony in our spirits, relationships, marriages, and homes. As Marley sings, we will be writing "songs of freedom."[6] And I say, with our own *marrsing* mission choices, we will exist in flow as life plays its music to our *marrsing* lyrics.

When we increase our knowledge through *marrsing* power and begin exercising control of our thoughts, feelings, actions, and behaviors, we enhance our interpersonal relationships, transform the way we relate and communicate our emotions.

MARRSING MISSION

Victory or defeat is in our thinking. Emotions don't think.
It's our thoughts that change because of the information
we receive, then it changes our feelings, which then
affects and dictates our moods and our emotions.

— Tony Evans

Living a *marrsing* mission life connects us with the purposes of our life and God. Our mind is part of the signal receiving network that raises our level of thought consciousness. Money and material possessions are riches. Owning riches does not automatically make us feel wealthy, but we use our minds to create thoughts of abundance and turn our riches into wealth for enjoyment in our relationships, marriages, and lives.

We enrich ourselves and others when we live with intentionality and positivity. Napoleon Hill says, "Power grows out of ORGANIZED KNOWL-EDGE … through application."[1] The continual renewing of our mind is what changes our lives. If we do not spend quality time analyzing and organizing our thoughts, actions, and behaviors, then we will continue to exist with the timid or raging of our emotions that drives us toward extreme behavior.

A *marrsing DIG* helps us clean up and throw out the old, heavy stuff that weighs us down emotionally, mentally, and physically. Carrying this heaviness within us makes it harder for us to live, love, sing, dance, and laugh with a spirit of gratitude, abundance, and prosperity. To soar above life's challenges, we have to be light enough to fly. The term "featherweight" refers to the lightest amount of weight. Heavy things and people do not move easily. Airlines limit us to a certain amount of weight in our baggage so they can monitor the allowable weight capacity for optimum performance and efficiency. As a regular traveler, I have had many experiences with overweight luggage that I had to lighten by determining what was important enough to take with me and what I had to leave behind. We need to *DIG* into what is inside us to eliminate the excessive and depressing contents of our lives. This may be hard to do on our own, but there are professionals who can assist us.

Every one of us has had good and bad experiences. The heavy stuff is what makes us depressed and keeps us on the negative side of life. If we want to coexist and have harmonious relationships, we need to identify and assess the heavy things in our lives that are weighing us down and making us sad, angry, or depressed. Bad experiences that are not thoroughly processed will carry more weight. Too much weight will prevent us from soaring toward a higher spirit of living. Heaviness prevents us from reaching new heights in our relationships and marriages. A *marrsing DIG* is one resource for managing the heavy emotions within us.

We are supposed to live with a "mission" to accomplish rather than just exist. McKay and McKay write, "When you're a child, the world is filled with promise and possibility, and your sense of wonder is easily kindled."[2] We should be intentional about indulging in the beauty of being able to breathe and enjoy the opportune moments in the world that show up to take our breath away. If we lose our enthusiasm for our partner and the relationship, we should ask ourselves, Why did I lose it? This is a part of *DIG*(ging) into the experiences that influence our personal energies and the vibrational auras that we exude when we are with our partners.

As adults, it is important for us to intentionally indulge in experiences that pique our deeper childlike curiosity and sense of freedom. Brett & Kate McKay blogged, "As the years go by and we mature, we find that the world doesn't always operate as we hoped. We learn to be realistic, to manage our expectations. We put up walls. We trust less. We cloak ourselves in cynicism to mitigate the sting of future disappointments."[3] McKay and McKay further explained that we can "maintain a little more emotional richness in adulthood, without sacrificing the solid footing of maturity that's essential for making progress."[4] I strongly believe we need to include "timeout moments" to communicate with our inner being. We should dedicate quiet time in our day to bask in the stillness of our minds and spirits. To connect with our emotions, intuitive insights, and invite a sense of wonder for the greatness inside us. When we are constantly rushing from one task to the next without tuning in to our mind and body, we are missing the deeper level signals. Sometimes replacing our modern day social media activities with affirmations, prayer, meditation, and introspective reflection can do wonders in quieting our minds. Using Churchill as a model, McKay and McKay encourage us to strive to "reach places where [we have] the power and opportunity to exercise the full capacity of [our] energy and imagination."[5]

Each chapter in our lives leads to the next. As a popular saying goes, "Life is a marathon, not a sprint." Change, transition, and transformation take a mission mindset. Improving our minds will improve our *self* and ultimately our relationships. As McKay and McKay note, "An awesome adulthood won't arrive on your doorstep like a package from Amazon. Grownup life is flooded with many streams of responsibilities."[6] If we allow ourselves to live on autopilot, we will end up being burdened by all our challenges weighing us down.

Better ingredients produce better products, and we are the ingredients in our relationship. Allowing ourselves additional time to romance our thoughts can add flow and a vital sense of imagination into our busy lives and ultimately our relationships. Simply listening to our favorite songs, immersing ourselves in an interesting book, video, or taking small trips to new and unfamiliar places—even by way of a new route home or an unplanned detour—can create a sense of calmness and inner power to handle life's challenges.

Ways to lift our mood are just a click away on the radio. There is a song for every feeling we experience. Music has the power to take us on emotional journeys and transport us to different places. The complexities of our individual selves, our hearts, and our lives have been evolving for years. Every relationship challenge or scenario we experience, someone else has endured. There is a song with lyrics that fit any circumstance, one that will lift our spirits from what we are going through. Positive song lyrics can elevate our moods and offer affirming words as we transform our minds and our actions toward enjoying more harmonious relationships.

Indulging in the plethora of rhythmic expressions available to us can unblock our flow. One of my favorite songs I use to redirect my thoughts of worry into faith and hope is Bob Marley and The Wailer's song "Three Little Birds." Marley sings, "Don't worry about a thing/'cause every little thing is gonna be alright."[7] Whenever I see birds flying, I am reminded of the Bible scripture Matthew 6:25–26 that I'll paraphrase here: "Therefore I say to you do not worry ... Look at the birds of the air ... our heavenly Father feeds them." God uses every one of us for his works. Some of us will plant seeds of life, some of us will water and nurture the seeds. Artists are our special universal seeds of expression; we should support and enjoy their talents. We should be open to listen and vibe to various genres of music to soothe our soul. We all have our favorite genres and artists based on preference, culture, ethnicity or ancestry, but we should be curious enough to step out of our limiting boundaries and expand our musical tastes. The world holds an abundance of musical rhythms and sounds for us to sample. Upbeat and positive music has magical powers and healing abilities to transform our minds, spirits, and bodies to joyful places without leaving where we are. We should sing along, even if we make up our own words. Let the music move us to our own sacred space of gratitude and renewal.

I enjoy dancing. Sometimes I get into a euphoric, mind elevating state simply by just dancing. Dancing and singing demand a state of flow. Happy people dance. Happiness is a choice we get to make even when circumstances are not ideal. Our ability to choose means we have options. Are we being intentional about the "state of being" we want to experience? Remember, holding on to negative emotions blocks our positive flow. Sadness comes from carrying around too many negative emotions that add weight around our ankles and stiffness in our hips. Sad emotions end up robbing us of our rhythm and keeping us stuck. They prevent us from moving freely and rhythmically to the music of life. When was the last time you danced? How are you surviving through the storms of your life and relationship?

American philosopher and psychologist, William James, writes that, "We shouldn't close-out on actively living and experiencing happiness while we're still alive."[8] We must stay open to all the possibilities that the universe offers us and the new paths of opportunity that life will lead us down. Living is more than just breathing. James also says, "Happiness is created as a result of us being active participants in the game of life. Instead of brooding about the suffering and evils of existence, we should re-adjust our attitudes and act as if life has an ultimate meaning … Believe that life is worth living, and your very belief will help you create the fact."[9] Happiness looks different for each of us at different times in our lives and relationships. What makes us happy is not someone else's responsibility or prerogative. We should define and create our own happiness and own it, despite the "talk" of other people or from our partners.

Thoughts are powerful! They manifest into how we behave. Our behaviors need to align with our intentions to experience the quality and harmony we desire. Kehoe says, "The problems and obstacles we encounter in life are caused by what is within us ... when we change our lens, our reality will change."[10] Positive thoughts energize us, and negative thoughts drain the life out of us and our relationships. We get to direct our energy toward feeding the thoughts that will become the strongest in our minds. Our energies manifest into our behaviors. The energy flow of our thoughts and actions either feeds or starves our relationship. We can use the power of *marrsing* to be intentional about how to respond rather than react. We must not verbalize thoughts with negativity, but instead choose positivity to create clear and intentional communication patterns in our relationships.

The force of *marrsing* can empower us. With the power of *marrsing*, we replace negative thoughts with positive and empowering ones that lead to constructive actions. Leading to behaviors that will move us toward experiencing peace within and a wealth of harmony in our relationships with our partners. Internationally known speaker and motivational coach Bob Proctor says, "We are already rich, some of us in money, relationships, health, love, or material possessions, but our capacity to recognize our richness lies within our mindset of scarcity, limitations, or abundance."[11] We have to start changing our mindset and begin thinking about how we can achieve the committed relationships that we desire.

Marrsing Thought

Love & Music transcends race, culture, creed, and continents; use them to create our own marrsing vibes in our life.

Angella Watkis Francis

MARRSING SUCCESS

Success is based upon power. Power is organized effort.

— Napoleon Hill

*Success is the development of the power with which
to get whatever one wants in life without interfering
with the rights of others.*

— Napoleon Hill

Throughout our daily lives, we plant seeds for future generations. Whether we realize it or not, everything we do matters. Every time we persevere in our purpose, every time we are true with our intentions, every time we serve others, we are making a difference. American inventor, co-founder, and former CEO of Apple Computers Steve Jobs inspired Stanford University graduates by telling them, "Your time is limited, so don't waste it living someone else's life. Don't be trapped by dogma—which is living with the results of other people's thinking. Don't let the noise of others' opinions drown out your own inner voice. And most important, have the courage to follow your heart and intuition."[1] We are the only ones who can live our lives. No one else has the answers that we have within us. No one else will consistently give the required effort to achieve what we want for ourselves. We must find time to be still and listen to our intuition and acknowledge the guiding spirit hovering around us with directional energy. Our thoughts and actions regarding what a successful, harmonious relationship feels like for us must align; we cannot listen to someone else's vision or opinion. Success is multifaceted. We should live our own success, not someone else's. I can assure you, owning your success feels much more fulfilling.

To follow our purpose in a way that improves our circumstance, we must reform our mental attitude and be intentional about what we allow to occupy our thoughts. We control what we let into our minds and who we allow to stay in our lives. We must take charge and guard our thoughts from negative influences. Whatever we take in, we have to let out at some point. With caution, we need to be mindful of who we listen to, what we watch, eat, drink, and what we allow into our spirit. What is inside of us will change our thoughts and actions. Occasionally, to find the answers within, we have to ask ourselves, "What's influencing our internal dialogue now? What are our thoughts saying about ourselves and our partners right now?"

As we embark on this transformative journey of living with a *marrsing* mission, we will develop a more positive outlook for our relationships. We will practice gratitude through life's adversities, defeats, and failures, which are all a part of building character, resilience, and appreciation for what is coming as more conscious individuals and partners. Dale Carnegie, best-selling author of the book *How to Stop Worrying & Start Living* writes, "A well-known legal maxim says: *De minimis non curat lex*- 'the law does not concern itself with trifles.' And neither should the worrier—if he wants peace of mind."[2] Continuing, Carnegie summarizes practical principles with rules on how to "break the worry habit before it breaks you." Rule two states, "Let's not allow ourselves to be upset by small things we should despise and forget. Remember, life is too short to be little." We must not worry about our partner's behavior; we have no control over their thoughts or actions. Instead, we need to direct our energy inward to clear blockages so we can experience positive flow, which influences harmony and helps us achieve success in our relationships.

We must pause and deliberate before we decide. Bishop Bronner tells us, "Our decisions determine our conduct, character and destiny ... [we must] think about the future consequences of our current decision."[3] Using the *marrsing pause* tool, we can take time to thoughtfully assess the state of our emotions and the value of what we are risking before we act or release any hurtful, mean-spirited, and damaging words out into the universe. We must not plant seeds of negativity because they will produce a negative harvest.

After we have dealt with the emotional insecurities, scars, and traumas of our past, we will no longer be imprisoned by a wounded mind. No longer will we internalize and exude the negative, toxic thoughts and behaviors associated with our traumatic experiences. A healthy love relationship creates positive bursts of universal life energies that ignite sparks of passion, romance, and adventure.

We must consistently remind our *selves* of the purpose and mutual goals of our committed relationships. We need to ask ourselves this question to help determine our choices: "Will these words and actions add, multiply, or subtract from the future relationship that I desire?" Then we must act according to what aligns with our desired result.

Marrsing Thought

Moving forward requires both bicycle wheels to spin just like the two partners in a marriage; they have to be in movement in the same direction in sync and harmony.

Angella Watkis Francis

MARRSING WISDOM

Revolutionary change fundamentally transforms our thoughts and beliefs. Rumbling with our story and owning our truth in order to write a new, more courageous ending transforms who we are and how we engage with the world.

— Brené Brown

The heart of the prudent acquires knowledge.

— Proverbs 8:16

As we embark on our *marrsing* mission of transforming into a more conscious version of ourselves as individuals and as partners, we need to use wisdom. Dyer tells us, "Learning a new task requires training your body to perform as your thoughts desire ... Wisdom combined with discipline fosters your ability to focus and be patient as you harmonize your thoughts, your intellect, and your feelings with the work of your body."[1] And Assaraf adds, "It takes effort, natural effort to change the propensity of the brain. As adults, we have to unlearn some things we've learned in the past."[2] These quotes especially pertain to beliefs and behaviors that are destructive and counterproductive to who we aspire to become.

Marrsing opens up great possibilities for us to start making conscious decisions to improve ourselves and our relationships. Assaraf notes, "We have to master our emotions and upgrade our skills so we can improve and upgrade our behaviors ... As human beings we don't always welcome change easily."[2] I once saw these funny-but-true words on a bumper sticker: "Only babies with wet diapers like change." We must begin to spark change from the roots of who we are and all the interconnected parts that feed into our current state of *self*. Assaraf posits, "All grown oak trees are interconnected down through their root system. An old oak tree can have root connections over a mile long underground."[3] Like a grown oak tree, adults have deep roots. These roots are made from personal experiences, cultural heritage, history, and other influences. *DIG*(ging) is integral to our self-evolution and growth. It can be an arduous mission but comes with a rewarding accomplishment.

Assaraf continues by saying, "To change is to grow. We are conditioned to be more of the same, so we don't want to change once we get comfortable."[4] In our quest to upgrade to a higher consciousness and become better versions of ourselves, we have to tap into our inner power. We need to defeat the "negative inner voice" that limits us. We have to release the negative past experiences that chain us to the anchor of stagnation and failure.

Author David Foster Wallace stated in his 2005 commencement address at Kenyon College that, "The ability to construct meaning from experiences is one of the most important skills."[5] I chose to use my experience from almost four decades of commitment, devotion, and love to share, teach, and inspire others to value their lives and relationships. *Marrsing* transforms and enhances our relationships and marital experiences if we want to live in harmony and enjoy more intimate moments.

The disintegration of my marriage became the "wind beneath my wings." It led me to pursue my life passion of sharing wisdom and valuable experiences so I could contribute to the betterment of intimate partner relationships and marriages. We must not let the disappointments in life hold us down. We should take all the time we need to acknowledge, process, and refocus. I am reassured by the Bible in Revelations 21:5, which says, "He who sat on the throne said, Behold, I make all things new. And He said to me 'Write, for these words are true and faithful.'" Sometimes we have to press the restart button.

The aspirational goals we achieve in life come from the strength of our passion and the level of tenacity we put into our efforts. We have to continue to pray, have faith, and trust God as we go through challenges. To help us move forward, we must learn to find the lessons in all situations and frame them as experiences in our life journey. We have to figure out what we can take from the experiences and find ways to use them going forward. To do this, we trust and believe that God is working on renewing our minds each day with every new possibility. The questions I think we should ask ourselves are: "What will I do with the experiences that have shaped my life? Will I use them to unlock greater abundances? Or will I allow them to negatively block my flow?

We are offered a new beginning every morning we wake up. Each new day brings fresh opportunities to reshape and redirect our thoughts and behaviors. It offers new possibilities to enhance and transform our relationships with the people we value most and have chosen to share our intimate space and moments with.

We should all be open to exploring all of life's enriching experiences that raise our energy levels and flow into our relationships. Let us be curious! Curiosity opens our minds to the wealth of knowledge and wisdom in the universe.

Unlocking our *marrsing* power changes how we manage our thoughts and actions. It allows us to begin directing our thoughts toward intentional contemplation of enhancing our connections and helps us become architects of our lives, marriages, and relationships. The *marrsing* path leads to valuable wisdom. We need to take the time to *DIG* into our past experiences to understand the blueprint of our authentic *selves*.

German-born physicist and winner of the 1921 Nobel Prize, Albert Einstein said, "Imagination is more important than knowledge. Knowledge is limited. Imagination encircles the world."[6] Our imagination can take us to faraway places. Our imaginations fuel our dreams, our dreams drive our motivations, and our motivations give us the momentum to take action toward the goals that contribute to our intentional purpose. This process rewards us with wealthy endeavors of richness, peace, and harmony and leads us toward becoming encapsulated in our knowledge, logic, and aspirations—for both our *selves* and our relationships.

Positive emotions enrich our mind and our state of wealth. Positivity nurtures us to grow, improve, and increase. Negative emotions rob our mind and spirit of its nurturing ability. Negativity leads us on a path of depletion and destruction. In his book *Think and Grow Rich*, Napoleon Hill writes, "the subconscious mind is more susceptible to influence by impulses of thought mixed with 'feelings' or emotion than by those originating solely in the reasoning portion of the mind." He goes on to say, "There are seven major positive emotions and seven major negative emotions. The negatives voluntarily inject themselves into the thought impulses, ensuring their passage into the subconscious mind. The positive must be injected through autosuggestion [self suggestion] into the thought." He shares two lists of the major positive and negative emotions, so know which ones to achieve and which ones to avoid:

"The Seven Major Positive Emotions:
- ❀ The emotion of DESIRE
- ❀ The emotion of FAITH
- ❀ The emotion of LOVE
- ❀ The emotion of SEX
- ❀ The emotion of ENTHUSIASM
- ❀ The emotion of ROMANCE
- ❀ The emotion of HOPE

The Seven Major Negative Emotions:
- ❀ The emotion of FEAR
- ❀ The emotion of JEALOUSY
- ❀ The emotion of HATRED
- ❀ The emotion of REVENGE
- ❀ The emotion of GREED
- ❀ The emotion of SUPERSTITION
- ❀ The emotion of ANGER"[7]

Our emotions determine how much wealth we perceive in our minds and enjoy in our lives. John Hagee, senior pastor and televangelist says, "A man or woman who enjoys what they have is wealthy."[8] Wealth is not measured by how much we have but by how little or how much we need to be content. It is our positivity and gratitude that increases or decreases our sense of wealth and value. When we unselfishly share and give of ourselves and our possessions, we are living, loving, and sharing as mediums of flow. We are acting as a vessel for God so he can pour his wisdom into us. Remember, what we have within us is what flows into our relationships. We should *DIG* in occasionally to check our flow and check what is emanating from our thoughts, spirits, and minds.

Only when we uncover the true source of our emotions can we consciously and knowledgeably chart the course of our own success in our lives and relationships. "An educated person," Hill states, "is not necessarily one who has an abundance of general or specialized knowledge. Educated people have developed the faculties of their minds so that they may acquire anything they want, or its equivalent, without violating the rights of others."[9]

He explains the origin of the word *educate* as deriving from the Latin word *educo*, meaning "to draw out or develop from within." By using the wisdom of *marrsing*, we benefit from knowing that if we apply the passion it requires, we have the power within us to achieve our purpose.

MARRSING AFFIRMATION

*One could speculate that this process opens up the possibility
to reinvent yourself and move away from the status quo
or to overcome past traumatic events that
evoke anxiety and stress.*

— Christopher Bergland

Knowledge becomes power when we use it to manage situations in our lives. We can begin to practice using contemplative and intentional thoughts, actions, and behaviors in dealings with our partners. Regardless of our relationship status, we can incorporate *marrsing* into our everyday lives. The choice to change is within our power. We need to practice *marrsing* contemplation every day: pause, breathe, analyze! Let us continue being conscious about our individual energies and patterns that give us signals about our choices and allow us to be mindful about our interactions.

Begin affirming by saying: "As I embrace the power of *marrsing*, I will become a more conscious and mature version of myself. I am aligning my thoughts, feelings, and actions toward creating a more intentional, purpose-driven outcome for my relationship."

CHAPTER 31

MARRSING LIFE

How much willpower you have will be less of an issue,
if you're already motivated to do something.[1]

— Bridget Grenville-Cleave

Self-control, which is essential for Goal achievement,
is like a muscle—the more you exercise it, the stronger it gets.[2]

— Bridget Grenville-Cleave

The Power of *marrsing* gives us energy to consciously enhance and transform our interpersonal connections by living, loving, and sharing from our authentic *selves*. In order to hone the transformational journey of *marrsing*, we have to decide to begin acting and living differently. We can start by pledging to identify a definite purpose that we will align with our actions and use it to achieve our true, long-term desires and goals. Then we can acknowledge our innate power through higher conscious awareness and spiritual guidance. Ignite our passion by recognizing the available abundance we have within us. We get to feel gratitude for everything that is a part of our lives and relationships; we understand our worth, and appreciate the value that our relationships offer us. We just have to tap into it all. In her book *Positive Psychology: A Practical Guide*, psychologist and author Bridget Grenville-Cleave writes, "Research into people's commitment to their goals suggests that it makes a difference to your self-motivation whether you focus on the progress you've already made towards your goal, or whether you focus on the things that you have left to achieve … Goals which are intrinsically motivating by definition need less self-control. Therefore, if you can find ways to improve your self-motivation, you won't need to worry so much about your willpower!"[1]

Let us repeat and adopt these *marrsing* affirmations as a personal, motivational pledge to ourselves and to our relationships:

- ✿ **Live Intentionally:** I will be open to the flow of life's opportunities and possibilities that feed my purpose. I will indulge in the abundance of the universe while honoring God's will for my relationship and life. I will live in gratitude and find enjoyment in each day.
- ✿ **Love Consciously:** I will allow the positive energies of affection and empathy to flow through me by acknowledging my emotions and being aware of the patterns in my life and relationships. I will initiate and reciprocate affection and empathy.
- ✿ **Share Generously:** I will create ways to be of service. I will seek out positivity and practice kindness. I will initiate and reciprocate compassion and appreciation.

Marrsing Thought

Marrsing Power is controlling our thoughts.
Not allowing our thoughts to take us aimlessly
where the 'others' are going or wants us to end up.

Angella Watkis Francis

MARRSING THOUGHTS

A higher level of consciousness elevates and
expands our mental capacity to own our truths.

Angella Watkis Francis

"I CAN'T" is one of the most self-defeating
phrases you can ever utter about your abilities
before actually trying.

Angella Watkis Francis

Having a wholehearted 'singleness' plays a major role in having a healthy and harmonious relationship.

Angella Watkis Francis

NOTES

CHAPTER 1: MARRSING COMMUNICATIONS

EPIGRAPH: Ralph S. Marston, Jr., "Perspectives of Others," The Daily Motivator, August 6, 2015, https://greatday.com/motivate/150806.html.

EPIGRAPH: James Allen, *As a Man Thinketh* in *The James Allen Collection* (San Francisco: Bottom of the Hill Publishing, 2010), 8.

1. Napoleon Hill, *Think and Grow Rich: The Landmark Bestseller—Now Revised and Updated for the 21st Century*, revised and expanded by Dr. Arthur R. Pell (New York, NY: Penguin, 2005), 208.

2. Marcus Aurelius, *The Meditations*, translated by Meric Casaubon (Project Gutenberg, 2001). http://www.gutenberg.org/files/2680/2680-h/2680-h.htm.

3. Timeless Classic Books, "MEDITATIONS MARCUS AURELIUS ANTONINUS—Full Audio Book—Stoicism—Stoic Philosophy," YouTube, March 10, 2018, video, https://www.youtube.com/watch?v=2aoISjbpuwU.

4. Robert Kiyosaki, *Rich Dad Poor Dad* (Scottsdale: Plata Publishing, 2017), 56.

CHAPTER 2: PURPOSE: AN INTENTIONAL JOURNEY

EPIGRAPH: Joel Osteen, *Finishing Grace* (Lakewood Church September 9, 2014) Anointed Messages Sermon Notes (anointedmessagesnotes. blogspot.com).

EPIGRAPH: James Allen, *Above Life's Turmoil* in *The James Allen Collection* (San Francisco: Bottom of the Hill Publishing, 2010), 10.

1. Oprah Winfrey, *What I Know for Sure* (New York, NY: Flatiron Books, 2014), back cover.

Love Intuition from 13 to 31

EPIGRAPH: [John Kehoe], *All Thought Is Creative* ... The Powers of the Mind! (Law of Attraction)," YouTube, May 28, 2015, video, time stamp, https://www.youtube.com/watch?v=HqD8RtyUU00.

1. Vekmehel Ofkirr, "*Bruce Lipton The Biology of Belief Full Lecture*," YouTube, December 21, 2014, video, 2:31, https://www.youtube.com/watch?v=82ShSNuru6c.

2. Florence Scovel Shinn, *The Power of the Spoken Word* (Mansfield Centre, CT: Martino Publishing, 2016), 19.

3. Deepak Chopra, *The Book of Secrets*, read by Daniel Passer, (New York, NY: Random House Audio, 2004), Audible audio ed., 8 hr., 53 min.

4. Ralph Waldo Emerson, *Essays, First Series* (1841; Project Gutenberg, 2021), Book IV, https://www.gutenberg.org/files/2944/2944-h/2944-h. htm.

5. Wayne Dyer, *The Power of Intention: Learning to Co-create Your World Your Way*, Gift, Reissue edition, Carlsbad, CA: Hay House Inc., October 1, 2010, Kindle ed.

6. Woffammily [Dale Bronner], "Resurrection 2012 6 am," YouTube, April 9, 2012, video, 41:40, https://www.youtube.com/watch?v=OxFtNwBSiQ8. [Quoting Benjamin Franklin, *Poor Richard's Almanack*, (New York, NY: Doggett, 1851; Waterloo, IA: USC Publishing), 143.

CHAPTER 3: THE GIFT OF LOVE

EPIGRAPH: The Dalai Lama, *His Essential Wisdom*, ed. Carol Kelly-Gangi (New York, NY: Fall River Press, 2007), 20.

EPIGRAPH: Don Miguel Ruiz, *The Mastery of Love: A Practical Guide to the Art of Relationship* (A Toltec Wisdom Book), (San Rafael, CA: Amber-Allen publishing, 1999), 10.

1. Deepak Chopra, *The Spontaneous Fulfillment of Desire, Harnessing the Infinite Power of Coincidence* (New York, NY: Three Rivers Press, 2003), 202.

The Gift of Commitment

EPIGRAPH: Brett and Kate McKay, "The Churchill School of Adulthood: A Prerequisite Class on Becoming the Author of Your Own Life," *The Art of Manliness*, December 11, 2020, https://www.artofmanliness. com/articles/the-churchill-school-of-adulthood-a-prerequisite-class-on-becoming-the-author-of-your-own-life/.

1. The Dalai Lama, *His Essential Wisdom*, ed. Carol Kelly-Gangi (New York, NY: Fall River Press, 2007), 18.

Wealth in Relationships

EPIGRAPH: Oprah Winfrey, *Words That Matter: A Little Book of Life Lessons* (New York, NY: HarperCollins, 2010), 65.

1. Shannon V. McHugh, "Are You Faking Happiness?" *eCounseling*, April 7, 2019, https://www.e-counseling.com/depression/ are-you-faking-happiness/.

2. Oprah Winfrey, *Words That Matter: A Little Book of Life Lessons* (New York, NY: HarperCollins, 2010), 45.

3. Helen Fisher, *Anatomy of Love: A Natural History of Mating, Marriage, and Why We Stray* (New York, NY: W.W. Norton, 2016), 39.

CHAPTER 4: THE MARRSING JOURNEY: LIVING, LOVING, SHARING

EPIGRAPH: Napoleon Hill, *Think and Grow Rich: The Landmark Bestseller—Now Revised and Updated for the 21ˢᵗ Century*, revised and expanded by Dr. Arthur R. Pell (New York, NY: Penguin, 2005), 47.

EPIGRAPH: The Dalai Lama, *The Dalai Lama: His Essential Wisdom*, ed. Carol Kelly-Gangi, (New York, NY: Fall River Press, 2007), 20.

1. Dale Bronner (@BishopBronner), "Never stop learning because life never stops teaching." Twitter, July 29, 2018, 10:45 p.m. https://twitter.com/bishopbronner/status/1023761547406049282.

2. Eckhart Tolle, *The Power of Now: A Guide to Spiritual Enlightenment*, read by the author (Novato, CA: New World Library, 2000), Audible audio ed., 7 hr., 37 min.

CHAPTER 5: THE MARRSING ENERGY: PURPOSE, POWER, AND PASSION

EPIGRAPH: Wayne Dyer, *The Power of Intention: Learning to Co-create Your World Your Way*, Gift, Reissue edition, Carlsbad, CA: Hay House Inc., October 1, 2010, Kindle ed., 149.

EPIGRAPH: Napoleon Hill, *The Law of Success: The Master Wealth-Builder's Complete and Original Lesson Plan for Achieving Your Dreams*. Originally published 1928. (New York, NY: Penguin Publishing Group, 2008), 30.

1. Brené Brown, *Daring Greatly: How the Courage to Be Vulnerable Transforms the Way We Live, Love, Parent, and Lead* (New York, NY: Penguin Audio, 2019), 34.

2. Paulo Coelho, *The Alchemist*, read by Jeremy Irons (New York: Harper Audio, 2004), Audible audio ed., 4 hr.

CHAPTER 6: "I AM"—THE ENERGY OF MY ENVIRONMENT

EPIGRAPH: Phillip C. McGraw (Dr. Phil), *Life Strategies: Doing What Works, Doing What Matters* (New York, NY: Hyperion, 1999), 232.

EPIGRAPH: John Assaraf, "How to Train Your Brain to Achieve Success – John Assaraf," YouTube, May 22, 2018, video, https://www.youtube. com/watch?v=GoC9HCnaF_8.

1. Viktor Frankl, Man's Search For Meaning (Boston, MA Beacon Press 2006), 72.

2. Wayne Dyer, *The Power of Intention: Learning to Co-create Your World Your Way*, Gift, Reissue edition, (Carlsbad, CA: Hay House Inc., October 1, 2010), Kindle ed. 154.

CHAPTER 7: PERSONAL POWER

EPIGRAPH: Napoleon Hill, *The Law of Success: The Master Wealth Builder's Complete and Original Lesson Plan for Achieving Your Dreams*. Originally published 1928. (New York, NY: Penguin Publishing Group, 2008), 30.

EPIGRAPH: James Allen, *The James Allen Collection: Above Life's Turmoil*, (San Francisco: Bottom of the Hill Publishing, 2010), 167.

1. Napoleon Hill, *The Law of Success: The Master Wealth Builder's Complete and Original Lesson Plan for Achieving Your Dreams*. Originally published 1928. (New York, NY: Penguin Publishing Group, 2008), 74.

2. James Allen, *The James Allen Collection: The Eight Pillars of Prosperity* (San Francisco: Bottom of the Hill Publishing, 2010), 210.

3. Ibid, *Above Life's Turmoil*, 167.

4. Deepak Chopra, *The Soul of Leadership: Unlocking Your Potential for Greatness*, read by the author (New York, NY: Random House Audio, 2010), Audible audio ed., 6 hr., 6 min.

CHAPTER 8: SOWING SEEDS

EPIGRAPH: Mahatma Ghandi

1. Ralph Waldo Emerson, *Essays, First Series* (Originally published 1841; Project Gutenberg, 2021), 4, https://www.gutenberg.org/ files/2944/2944-h/2944-h.htm.

2. Dr. Arun Gandhi, Foreword to *Mahatma Gandhi: His Life and Ideas* by Charles F. Andrews (Woodstock, VT: Skylight Paths, 2007), xiv.

3. Bee EPiC Daily, "The Strangest Secret by Earl Nightingale (quality recording)," YouTube, June 23, 2019, video, https://www.youtube.com/watch?v=F4s1Fyh4HAg.

4. Dr. Henry Cloud and Dr. John Townsend, *Boundaries in Marriage* (Grand Rapids, MI: Zondervan, 1999), 32–33.

CHAPTER 9: BEING IN FLOW

EPIGRAPH: EliteBITLLIONAIRE'S M., "Become an Eagle and stop Surrounding yourself with Chickens," (Motivational speech by T. D. Jakes.) YouTube, November 22, 2017, video, https://www.youtube.com/watch?v=fQ4Rswqp_C8.

1. Bob Marley, "Redemption Song," recorded January–April 1980, track 10 on *Uprising*, Tuff Gong, compact disc.

2. Viktor Frankl, *Man's Search for Meaning* (Boston: Beacon Press, 2006), 104.

CHAPTER 10: THE COMMITTED SELF

EPIGRAPH: The Entheos Initiative, "The Strangest Secret Earl Nightingale 1956 Original FULL," YouTube, January 2, 2017, video, https://www.youtube.com/watch?v=PeW_DMV_3Wg.

CHAPTER 11: MARRSING VIBRATIONAL ENERGY

EPIGRAPH: Bob Marley, "Positive Vibration," recorded 1975–1976, track 1 on *Rastaman Vibration*, Tuff Gong, compact disc.

1. The Coconut Code, "The Strangest Secret in the World by Earl Nightingale full 1950," YouTube, January 1, 2015, video, https://www.youtube.com/watch?v=UygnXqoKrC4.

2. Tony Evans, "God Wants to Reveal Himself Through this Crisis," YouTube, May 18, 2020, video, 1:46, https://www.youtube.com/watch?v=fiKv_ZNTlPo.

3. Buju Banton, "Wanna Be Loved," recorded 1994–1995, track 11 on *'Til Shiloh*, Loose Canon/Island, compact disc.

CHAPTER 12: CREATING BOUNDARIES

EPIGRAPH: Brené Brown, *Rising Strong: How the Ability to Reset Transforms the Way We Live, Love, Parent, and Lead* (New York, NY: Random House, 2017), 129.

EPIGRAPH: Dr. Henry Cloud and Dr. John Townsend, *Boundaries in Marriage* (Grand Rapids, MI: Zondervan, 1999), 28.

1. Dr. Henry Cloud and Dr. John Townsend, *Boundaries in Marriage* (Grand Rapids, MI: Zondervan, 1999), 17.

2. Alduan Tartt, "True Talk: Dr Alduan Tartt and Bishop Dale Bronner (How to Have Better Relationships," YouTube, September 2, 2017, video, https://www.youtube.com/watch?v=nHDJe4GKeRI.

3. Dr. Henry Cloud and Dr. John Townsend, *Boundaries in Marriage* (Grand Rapids, MI: Zondervan, 1999), 11–12.

4. Ibid, 22.

5. His Holiness the 14th Dalai Lama of Tibet, "Non-Violence, the Appropriate and Effective Response to Human Conflicts," accessed February 28, 2021, https://www.dalailama.com/messages/world-peace/9-11.

6. Dr. Henry Cloud and Dr. John Townsend, *Boundaries in Marriage* (Grand Rapids, MI: Zondervan, 1999), 23.

CHAPTER 13: OUR RIGHT TO CHOOSE

EPIGRAPH: Gaither Music TV, "Wintley Phipps – It Is Well With My Soul [Live]," YouTube, April 6, 2012, video, https://www.youtube.com/watch?v=E8HffdyLd0c.

EPIGRAPH: Stephen Covey, *The Eighth Habit: From Effectiveness to Greatness*, read by the author (New York, NY: Simon & Schuster Audio, 2004), Audible audio ed., 14 hr. 23 min.

1. The Dalai Lama, *The Dalai Lama: His Essential Wisdom*, ed. Carol Kelly-Gangi, (New York, NY: Fall River Press, 2007), 42.

2. John Kehoe, *Secrets of the Subconscious Mind: The Easy Way to Create Success* (Secrets_of_the_Subconscious_Mind.pdf (mcusercontent.com) downloaded April 22, 2021), 2021), eBook ed., page 6.

3. Stephen Covey, *The Eighth Habit: From Effectiveness to Greatness*, read by the author (New York, NY: Simon & Schuster Audio, 2004), Audible audio ed., 14 hr., 23 min.

CHAPTER 14: DECIDING TO CHANGE

EPIGRAPH: John Kehoe, *Secrets of the Subconscious Mind: The Easy Way to Create Success* (PDF Version – John Kehoe – Secrets_of_the_ Subconscious_Mind.pdf 2021), eBook ed., page 6.
1. EliteBITLLIONAIRE'S M., "Become an Eagle and stop Surrounding yourself with Chickens," (Motivational speech by T. D. Jakes.) YouTube, November 22, 2017, video, https://www.youtube.com/ watch?v=fQ4Rswqp_C8.
2. Ibid.
3. Ibid.

CHAPTER 15: MARRSING DIG = DEEP INNER GRATITUDE

EPIGRAPH: John Kehoe, *Secrets of the Subconscious Mind: The Easy Way to Create Success* (John Kehoe – Secrets_of_the_Subconscious_Mind.pdf, 2021), eBook ed., page 10.
1. Jill Bolte Taylor, *My Stroke of Insight: A Brain Scientist's Personal Journey* (New York, NY: Penguin Audio Group USA; Unabridged edition (3 July 2008) Viking, 2008), Audio CD.
2. Stephen R. Covey, *Living the 7 Habits: The Courage to Change*, read by Stephen R. Covey (Grand Haven, MI: Brilliance Audio, 2015), audio CD, 1 hour and 13 minutes.
3. Tracy Smith, "Emotionally Unavailable Partners and How to Spot Them," June 2, 2019, https://www.e-counseling.com/relationships/ emotionally-unavailable-partners-and-how-to-spot-them/.
4. Brené Brown, *Rising Strong, How The Ability To Reset Transforms The Way We Live, Love, Parent and Lead*, p. 241.
5. Deepak Chopra, *The Soul of Leadership: Unlocking Your Potential for Greatness*, read by the author (New York, NY: Random House Audio, 2010), Audible audio ed., 6 hr., 6 min.

6.   Super Soul Sunday, season 10, episode 1, "Oprah & Author Richard Rohr: The Search For Our True Self," OWN, aired February 8, 2015.

CHAPTER 16: GRATITUDE FOR GREATNESS WITHIN

EPIGRAPH: Thich Nhat Hanh, *Reconciliation: Healing the Inner Child* (Berkeley, CA: Parallax Press; October 9, 2006).

1.   Brené Brown, *Daring Greatly: How the Courage to Be Vulnerable Transforms the Way We Live, Love, Parent, and Lead*, read by the author (New York, NY: Penguin Audio, 2018), 226 & Audible audio ed., 6 hr., 30 min.

2.   Brett & Kate McKay, "The Churchill School of Adulthood: A Prerequisite Class on Becoming the Author of Your Own Life," *The Art of Manliness*, December 11, 2020, https://www.artofmanliness. com/articles/the-churchill-school-of-adulthood-a-prerequisite-class-on-becoming-the-author-of-your-own-life/.

3.   Brené Brown, *Daring Greatly: How the Courage to Be Vulnerable Transforms the Way We Live, Love, Parent, and Lead*, (New York, NY: Penguin, 2018), p. 110.

4.   Ibid. p. 231

5.   Ibid. p. 248

6.   Brett & Kate McKay, "The Churchill School of Adulthood – Lesson #3: Live Romantically," last modified June 3, 2021, https://www.artofmanliness.com/articles/the-churchill-school-of-adulthood-lesson-3-live-romantically/.

Declaring Who I Am

EPIGRAPH: Tony Evans, *Kingdom Single* – The Urban Alternative – Listen to The Alternative with Dr. Tony Evans, Sep 18, 2018 (oneplace.com).

1.   Andrea Miller, "Be Beautiful, Be Yourself," [an interview with Thich Nhat Hanh], *Shambhala Sun*, November 29, 2011, https://plumvillage. org/about/thich-nhat-hanh/interviews-with-thich-nhat-hanh/ shambhala-sun-january-2012/.

2. Neville Goddard, *The Power of Awareness* (New York, NY: Penguin Random House/TarcherPerigree, 2012), 6, The Power of Awareness: Neville Goddard: 9781603865043: Amazon.com: Books.

3. Giving Voice to the Wisdom of the Ages, "I AM Discourse St Germain 1–33 Complete," YouTube, October 19, 2019, Video, timestamp, https://www.youtube.com/watch?v=z5G0E2Qm6g4.

4. Myles Munroe, *Becoming a Leader: How to Develop and Release Your Unique Gifts* (New Kensington, PA: Whitaker House, 2018), 60.

5. Joseph Murphy, *The Power of Your Subconscious Mind* (New York, NY: Prentice Hall, 1994), Chp. *The Marvelous Power of Your Subconscious Mind:* The Power of Your Subconscious Mind – Kindle (amazon.com) The Power of Your Subconscious Mind by Joseph Murphy – Full Audio Book | Mind Power – (895) The Power of Your Subconscious Mind by Joseph Murphy – Full Audio Book | Mind Power – YouTube.

6. John Kehoe, *Secrets of the Subconscious Mind: The Easy Way to Create Success* (John Kehoe – Secrets_of_the_Subconscious_Mind.pdf, 2021), eBook ed.

7. Ibid, 6.

8. John Kehoe, "Changing Beliefs," n.d., John Kehoe Mind Power, an excerpt from Money, Success and You, a book by John Kehoe, https://www.learnmindpower.com/article/changing-beliefs/.

9. Super Soul Sunday, season 10, episode 1, "Oprah & Author Richard Rohr: The Search For Our True Self," OWN, aired February 8, 2015.

CHAPTER 17: MARRSING PAUSE

EPIGRAPH: Plato, *Apology*, translated by Benjamin Jowett (Internet Classics Archive, 2000), http://classics.mit.edu/Plato/apology.html.

1. Stephen Covey, *The 8ᵗʰ Habit: From Effectiveness to Greatness* (New York, NY: Simon & Schuster Audio, 2004), Audible audio ed., 14 hr., 23 min.

2. Rollo May, "Freedom and Responsibility Examined," in *Behavioral Science and Guidance: Proposals and Perspectives*, Esther Lloyd-Jones and

Esther M. Westervelt, eds., (New York, NY: Bureau of Publications, Teachers College, Columbia University, 1963), 5.

3.   Christopher Bergland, "Superfluidity: Decoding the Enigma of Cognitive Flexibility," *Psychology Today*, September 2, 2015, https://www.psychologytoday.com/us/blog/the-athletes-way/201509/superfluidity-decoding-the-enigma-cognitive-flexibility.

4.   Don Miguel Ruiz with Janet Mills, *The Voice of Knowledge, Story of My Life*, ed. Janet Mills (San Rafael, California: Amber-Allen Publishing 2004), 122.

5.   Viktor Frankl, *Man's Search For Meaning* (Boston: Beacon Press, 2006), 77, https://archive.org/details/manssearchformea00vikt.

6.   Dennis Brown, "How Could I Leave," released 1992, track 9 on *Live in Montego Bay*, Sonic Sounds, compact disc.

Words Have Power

1.   James Allen, "*Above Life's Turmoil*," in *The James Allen Collection* (San Francisco: Bottom of The Hill Publishing, 2010), 167.

2.   The Dalai Lama, *His Essential Wisdom*, ed. Carol Kelly-Gangi (New York, NY: Fall River Press, 2007), 116.

3.   Power for Living with Bishop Dale C. Bronner, episode #SA080518, "Mouth Peace," Daystar Television Sunday, aired December 2, 2018.

4.   Thich Nhat Hanh, *Anger: Wisdom for Cooling the Flames* (New York, NY: Riverhead Books, 2002), (898) ANGER: Wisdom for Cooling the Flames | by Thich Nhat Hanh (Full Audiobook) – YouTube – Accessed 7/26/2021.

5.   Thich Nhat Hanh, *Anger: Wisdom for Cooling the Flames* Paperback – Deckle Edge, (Riverhead Books, New York, NY 2001) (898) ANGER: Wisdom for Cooling the Flames | by Thich Nhat Hanh (Full Audiobook) – YouTube Accessed 7/26/2021.

6.   Stevie Wonder, Quote: "*Mama was my greatest teacher …*" https://www.brainyquote.com/quotes/stevie_wonder_399917.

CHAPTER 18: CHALLENGES WILL COME

EPIGRAPH: Napoleon Hill, *Think and Grow Rich: The Landmark Bestseller—Now Revised and Updated for the 21ˢᵗ Century*, revised and expanded by Dr. Arthur R. Pell (New York, NY: TarcherPerigee, 2005), 26.

EPIGRAPH: Viktor Frankl, *Man's Search For Meaning* (Boston: Beacon Press, 2006), 112, https://archive.org/details/manssearchformea00vikt.

EPIGRAPH: Dale C. Bronner, Daystar Television Sunday. *Power for Living with Bishop Dale C. Bronner*. Episode #SA080518, "Mouth Peace," aired December 2, 2018. Daystar Television.

1. {Ibid. SA080518}
2. Super Soul Sunday. "Oprah and Dr. Gary Chapman: The Five Love Languages." November 20, 2019. Video, 21:38. https://omny.fm/shows/oprah-s-supersoul-conversations/oprah-and-dr-gary-chapman-the-five-love-languages.
3. Dale Bronner, *The Power of Choice—Power for Living with Bishop Dale C. Bronner*. Daystar Television Sunday. Video. Airdate: February 24, 2019.

What Marriage and Infidelity Mean to Us

EPIGRAPH: Pema Chodron, *Welcoming the Unwelcome*, read by Claire Foy (Berkley, CA: Shambhala Publications, 2009), Audible audio ed., 4 hr., 35 min.

1. Ellie Delano, " 'Capstone' Marriage vs 'Cornerstone Marriage' " *Woman's Day*, May 30, 2013, https://www.womansday.com/relationships/dating-marriage/a46635/capstone-vs-cornerstone-marriage/.
2. Esther Perel, *The State of Affairs: Rethinking Infidelity* (London: Yellow Kite, 2018), 19.
3. Ibid, 45.
4. Ibid, 32.
5. Ibid, 31.
6. Ibid, 30.

7. "Infidelity," American Association for Marriage and Family Therapy, last updated July 2016, https://www.aamft.org/Consumer_Updates/ Infidelity.aspx.

8. Marty Klein, *After the Affair … What?* Sexual Intelligence, Issue 164, October 2013, http://www.sexualintelligence.org/newsletters/issue164. html.

9. Ibid, 92.

10. The Dalai Lama, "Message from the H.H. The Dalai Lama," *Snow Lion* 16, no. 4 (2002), https://www.shambhala.com/wp/wp-content/ uploads/2017/03/60.pdf.

11. Esther Perel, *The State of Affairs: Rethinking Infidelity* (London: Yellow Kite, 2018), 152.

12. "Infidelity," American Association for Marriage and Family Therapy, last updated July 2016, https://www.aamft.org/Consumer_Updates/ Infidelity.aspx.

13. Mel Robbins, "Transform Your Life, Work and Confidence with Everyday Courage," March 28, 2019, Bay Path Women's Leadership Conference.

CHAPTER 19: SHARING AND SERVING IN OUR RELATIONSHIPS

EPIGRAPH: Patti LaBelle, *Don't Block the Blessings* (New York, NY: Riverhead, 1996).

1. Paulo Coelho, *The Alchemist*, read by Jeremy Irons (New York, NY: Harper Audio, 2004), Audible audio ed., 4 hr.

2. Gary Chapman, *The 5 Love Languages: How to Express Heartfelt Commitment to Your Mate*, read by the author (Carol Stream, IL: Oasis Audio, 2005), Audible audio ed., 4 hr., 46 min.

3. "Oh, Be Careful, Little Eyes, what you see," hymnal.net, https://www. hymnal.net/en/hymn/c/157.

4. Ralph Marston, *Curiosity* – The Daily Motivator, Monday, June 16, 2008, The Daily Motivator – Curiosity (greatday.com).

The Needs of Our Relationship

EPIGRAPH: Zig Ziglar – Quote: *"You can have everything in life you want, if you will just help enough other people get what they want."* Ziglar Inc – Personal Development Training, Sales Coaching – Plano, Texas.

1. Abraham Maslow, *Maslow's Hierarchy of Needs Explained* – By Elizabeth Hopper Updated February 24, 2020 part #7 Love and Belonging Maslow's Hierarchy of Needs Explained (thoughtco.com).

2. Gary Chapman, *The 5 Love Languages: How to Express Heartfelt Commitment to Your Mate*, read by the author (Carol Stream, IL: Oasis Audio, 2005), Audible audio ed., 4 hr., 46 min.

3. Gospel Portal, "Bishop Dale C Bronner Release Your Decree," YouTube, March 23, 2013, video, https://www.youtube.com/watch?v=kWooYY4rpBk.

CHAPTER 20: CAUSES OF DISHARMONY IN RELATIONSHIPS

EPIGRAPH: Joel Osteen, *Your Best Life Begins Each Morning: Devotions to Start Every Day of the Year* (New York, NY: FaithWords, 2008), 90.

EPIGRAPH: Brett and Kate McKay, "The Churchill School of Adulthood: A Prerequisite Class on Becoming the Author of Your Own Life," *The Art of Manliness*, December 11, 2020, https://www.artofmanliness.com/articles/the-churchill-school-of-adulthood-a-prerequisite-class-on-becoming-the-author-of-your-own-life/.

1. Esther Perel, *The State of Affairs: Rethinking Infidelity* (London: Yellow Kite, 2018), 30.

2. Ibid, 10.

3. Ibid, 14.

4. James Allen, *As a Man Thinketh* in *The James Allen Collection* (San Francisco: Bottom of the Hill Publishing, 2010), 151 & 155.

5. Henry Cloud & John Townsend, *Boundaries in Marriage*, (New York, NY MJF Books 1999), 147.

6. Earl Nightingale, *The Strangest Secret*, read by the author and Vic Conant (Wheeling, IL: Nightingale-Conant, 2014), Audible audio ed., 1 hr., 46 min.

7. Bishop Dale C. Bronner, *Power To Choose*, Power For Living – televised sermon.

8. Bishop Dale C. Bronner, *Power To Choose*, Power For Living – televised sermon.

9. SuperSoul Conversations Podcast by Oprah, "Oprah's SuperSoul Conversations Podcast – Pastor A. R. Bernard: Four Things Women Want from a Man," YouTube, September 11, 2017, video, 38:23, https://www.youtube.com/watch?v=gL4ru4qXnhE.

Character and Influences

EPIGRAPH: James Allen, *As a Man Thinketh*, The James Allen Free Library, accessed March 1, 2021 http://james-allen.in1woord.nl/?text=as-a-man-thinketh.

1. Woffamily, "Look at the Birds, Bishop Dale C. Bronner, Word of Faith Family Worship Cathedral," YouTube, March 19, 2020, video, 56:00, https://www.youtube.com/watch?v=su0mo-wp81Q.

2. Terry and Barbi Franklin, "You Can Tell a Lot About a Man," released 2006, track 10 on *Songs of Love and Marriage*, Tylis Music Group, compact disc.

3. Earl Nightingale, *Lead the Field*, read by the author (Wheeling, IL: Nightingale-Conant, 2018), Audible audio ed., 2 hr., 44 min.

4. Plato, *Apology*, translated by Benjamin Jowett (Internet Classics Archive, 2000), http://classics.mit.edu/Plato/apology.html.

CHAPTER 21: DISEMPOWERING RELATIONSHIPS

1. Michele Overman, "How to Identify and Deal with Passive-Aggressive People," June 1, 2019, https://www.e-counseling.com/relationships/how-to-identify-and-deal-with-passive-aggressive-people/.

2. J. Martin Kohe, *Your Greatest Power*, read by Christopher Lane ©1953 Original Edition (c) by The Napoleon Hill Foundation. Revised Edition (c) 2004 by The Napoleon Hill Foundation (P) 2014 Brilliance Audio, all rights reserved. (Brilliance Audio 2014), Audible audio ed., 1 hr., 37 min.

CHAPTER 22: EMOTIONAL ENTANGLEMENTS AND COLLISIONS: OUR PARTNER'S PSYCHE AND PERSONALITY

1. DoctorRamani, "What's Gaslighting? (Individual, tribe, and societal gaslighting) – Dr. Ramani Durvasula," YouTube. April 22, 2019. Video, 11:42, https://www.youtube.com/watch?v=UTS5XsZe9Jg.
2. Michelle Overman, "How to Identify and Deal with Passive-Aggressive People," June 1, 2019, https://www.e-counseling.com/relationships/how-to-identify-and-deal-with-passive-aggressive-people/.
3. Ibid, para.8 – *Be Open To Their Feelings*.
4. Ibid, para. 8 – *Be Open To Their Feelings*.
5. Tracy Smith, "Emotionally Unavailable Partners and How to Spot Them," June 2, 2019, https://www.e-counseling.com/relationships/emotionally-unavailable-partners-and-how-to-spot-them/.par#4 – *Intense Anger*.

CHAPTER 23: MANAGING OUR CHANGE

EPIGRAPH: Eckhart Tolle, *The Power of Now: A Guide to Spiritual Enlightenment*, read by the author (Novato, CA: New World Library, 2000), Audible audio ed., 7 hr., 37 min.

1. Bob Marley, "Redemption Song," recorded January–April 1980, track 10 on *Uprising*, Tuff Gong, compact disc.
2. Bob Marley, "Trenchtown Rock," recorded 1971, originally released as track 1 on *Live!*, TuffGong, compact disc.
3. "The Music Instinct: Science and Song," DVD, directed by Elena Mannes, (Alexandria, VA: PBS, 2009).
4. Maya Angelou, Twitter Post, May 22nd, 2021, 10:45 AM. https://twitter.com/DrMayaAngelou/status/1396115035273957381.
5. Katherine Hurst, The Secret Law of Attraction: Master The Power of Intention (London, Greater Minds 2016) http://www.thelawofattraction.com/6-steps-to-begin-using-creative-visualization/.

CHAPTER 24: PRESERVING OUR RELATIONSHIPS AND OUR ENVIRONMENT

1. Bridget Grenville-Cleave, *Positive Psychology: A Practical Guide* (New York, NY: MJF Books, 2012), 123.

CHAPTER 25: MARRSING CLAUSE

1. Cy Wakeman, "Name of Session," March 2019, Bay Path University's 24th Annual Women's Leadership Conference in Springfield, Massachusetts.
2. Eleanor Roosevelt, The Faith of a First Lady: Eleanor Roosevelt's Spirituality – Truman Library Institute, Dr. Harold Ivan Smith, https://www.trumanlibraryinstitute.org/library-events/.
3. Dale Bronner, *The Pursuit of Happiness* – Power For Living, The Pursuit of Happiness – TRUE WORD OF YESHUA.
4. Ibid.

CHAPTER 26: MARRSING ON THE BRAIN – A JOURNEY OF SUCCESS

1. Courtney E. Ackerman, "What is Neuroplasticity? A Psychologist Explains," positivepsychology.com, May 2, 2021, https://positivepsychology.com/neuroplasticity/.
2. Napoleon Hill, *The Law of Success, The Master Wealth-Builder's **Complete and Original** Lesson Plan for Achieving Your Dreams (New York, NY, Penguin 2008)*, 39.
3. John Assaraf, *How to Set and Achieve Your Goals* [3 parts to our habits] – (898) How to Set and Achieve Any Goal You Have in Your Life – John Assaraf (Part 1) – YouTube.
4. Mathieu Servant, Peter Casey, & Geoffrey F. Woodman, "Neural Bases of Automaticity," *Journal of Experimental Psychology: Learning, Memory, and Cognition 44*, no. 3, (2018): 440–464, https://doi.org/10.1037/xlm0000454.

5. Kaihan Krippendorff, "Universal Law: Repeat What You Want and You Will Get It," Kaihan Krippendorff (blog), January 23, 2017, https://kaihan.net/universal-law-repeat-want-will-get/.

6. Bob Marley, "Redemption Song," recorded January–April 1980, track 10 on *Uprising*, Tuff Gong, compact disc.

CHAPTER 27: MARRSING MISSION

1. Napoleon Hill, *Napoleon Hill, The Law of Success, The Master Wealth-Builder's **Complete and Original** Lesson Plan for Achieving Your Dreams* (New York, NY, Penguin 2008), 39.

2. Brett and Kate McKay, "The Churchill School of Adulthood – Lesson #3: Live Romantically," last modified June 3, 2021, https://www.artofmanliness.com/articles/the-churchill-school-of-adulthood-lesson-3-live-romantically/.

3. Brett and Kate McKay, "The Churchill School of Adulthood – Lesson #3: Live Romantically," last modified June 3, 2021, https://www.artofmanliness.com/articles/the-churchill-school-of-adulthood-lesson-3-live-romantically/.

4. Ibid, *Takeaways From Lesson #3*.

5. Ibid, *Takeaways From Lesson #3*.

6. Brett and Kate McKay, "The Churchill School of Adulthood: A Prerequisite Class on Becoming the Author of Your Own Life," *The Art of Manliness*, June 3, 2021, https://www.artofmanliness.com/articles/the-churchill-school-of-adulthood-a-prerequisite-class-on-becoming-the-author-of-your-own-life/.

7. Brett and Kate McKay, "The Churchill School of Adulthood Conclusion: Thought + Action = An Awesome Adulthood," *The Art of Manliness*, June 6, 2021, https://www.artofmanliness.com/articles/churchill-conclusion/

8. Brett and Kate McKay, "The Churchill School of Adulthood: A Prerequisite Class on Becoming the Author of Your Own Life," *The Art of Manliness*, June 3, 2021, https://www.artofmanliness.com/articles/the-churchill-school-of-adulthood-a-prerequisite-class-on-becoming-the-author-of-your-own-life/.

9. Bob Marley and The Wailers, "Three Little Birds," recorded 1977, track 9 on *Exodus*, TuffGong, compact disc.

10. William James, *Pragmatism and Other Writings* (New York, NY: Penguin Classics, 2000), 240.

11. Ibid, 240.

CHAPTER 28: MARRSING SUCCESS

EPIGRAPH: Napoleon Hill, *The Law of Success – The Master Wealth Builder's Complete and Original Lesson Plan for Achieving Your Dreams.* Originally published 1928. (New York, NY: Penguin Publishing Group, 2008), 69.

EPIGRAPH: Ibid, 74.

1. Stanford News, " 'You've got to find what you love,' Jobs Says," June 12, 2005, https://news.stanford.edu/2005/06/14/jobs-061505/.

2. Dale Carnegie, *Dale Carnegie's Lifetime Plan for Success: How to Win Friends and Influence People & How to Stop Worrying and Start Living,* (New York, NY: Galahad Books, 1998), 310.

3. Bishop Dale C. Bronner, "The Power for Living: Future Consequences of Current Decisions [SA110418]," Station: Daystar Television, 12/2/2018.

CHAPTER 29: MARRSING WISDOM

EPIGRAPH: Brené Brown, *Rising Strong: How the Ability to Reset Transforms the Way we Live, Love, Parent and Lead,* (New York, NY, Random House, 2017), 41.

1. Wayne Dyer, *The Power of Intention: Learning to Co-create Your World Your Way*, Gift, Reissue edition, Carlsbad, CA: Hay House Inc., October 1, 2010, Kindle ed., 12.

2. John Assaraf, How to Train Your Brain to Achieve Success – Streamed May 22, 2018 – Accessed November 18, 2018 (904) How to Train Your Brain to Achieve Success – John Assaraf – YouTube.

3. Ibid, Video – How to Train Your Brain to Achieve Success – Streamed May 22, 2018.

4. Ibid, Video – How to Train Your Brain to Achieve Success – Streamed May 22, 2018.

5. Ibid, Video – How to Train Your Brain to Achieve Success – Streamed May 22, 2018.

6. Lynn Skittle, "This Is Water – Full version-David Foster Wallace Commencement Speech," YouTube, May 19, 2013, video, 22:43, https://www.youtube.com/watch?v=8CrOL-ydFMI.

7. Napoleon Hill, *Think and Grow Rich: The Landmark Bestseller—Now Revised and Updated for The 21ˢᵗ Century*, revised and expanded by Dr. Arthur R. Pell (New York, NY: Quarto Books, 2015) 233–235.

8. Hagee Ministries, "The Portrait of the Mother," YouTube, May 9, 2021, video, 28:45. (Originally aired on 1/14/2018 as a TBN broadcast.)

9. Napoleon Hill, *Think and Grow Rich: The Landmark Bestseller—Now Revised and Updated for the 21ˢᵗ Century*, revised and expanded by Dr. Arthur R. Pell (New York, NY: Penguin, 2005), 80.

CHAPTER 31: CONCLUSION-MARRSING LIFE

1. Bridget Grenville-Cleave, *Positive Psychology; A Practical Guide* (New York, NY: MJF Books, 2012), 123.

2. Ibid, 123.

BIBLIOGRAPHY

Ackerman, Courtney E. "What is Neuroplasticity? A Psychologist Explains." Positivepsychology.com. May 2, 2021. https://positivepsychology.com/neuroplasticity/.

Allen, James. *The James Allen Collection*. San Francisco: Bottom of the Hill Publishing, 2010.

Angelou, Maya. Quote – Facebook Post – August 25, 2010 (20+) Maya Angelou | Facebook.

Assaraf, John. (Additional source).

Assaraf, John. "Deliberate Conscious Evolution – Means we can change the neuropathy of our brains to change our habits." Neurogym.

Assaraf, John. "How to Train Your Brain to Achieve Success – John Assaraf." YouTube. May 22, 2018. Video, 46:27. https://www.youtube.com/watch?v=GoC9HCnaF_8.

Aurelius, Marcus. *The Meditations*. Translated by Meric Casaubon. Project Gutenberg, 2001. http://www.gutenberg.org/files/2680/2680-h/2680-h.htm.

Banton, Buju. "Wanna Be Loved." Recorded 1994–1995. Loose Canon/Island, compact disc.

Bee EPiC Daily. "The Strangest Secret by Earl Nightingale (quality recording)." YouTube. June 23, 2019. Video, 35:02. https://www.youtube.com/watch?v=F4s1Fyh4HAg.

Bergland, Christopher. "Superfluidity: Decoding the Enigma of Cognitive Flexibility." *Psychology Today*, September 2, 2015. https://www.psychologytoday.com/us/blog/the-athletes-way/201509/superfluidity-decoding-the-enigma-cognitive-flexibility.

Bronner, Dale C. "The Power for Living: Future Consequences of Current Decisions [SA110418]." Daystar Television, 12/2/2018.

Bronner, Dale (@BishopBronner). "Never stop learning because life never stops teaching." Twitter, July 29, 2018. https://twitter.com/bishopbronner/status/1023761547406049282.

Brown, Brené. *Daring Greatly: How the Courage to Be Vulnerable Transforms the Way We Live, Love, Parent, and Lead.* New York, NY: Avery, 2015.

Brown, Brené. *Rising Strong: How the Ability to Reset Transforms the Way We Live, Love, Parent and Lead.* New York, NY: Random House, 2017.

Brown, Dennis. "How Could I Leave." Released 1992. Sonic Sounds, compact disc.

Carnegie, Dale. *Dale Carnegie's Lifetime Plan for Success: How to Win Friends and Influence People & How to Stop Worrying and Start Living.* New York, NY: Galahad Books, 1998.

Chapman, Gary. *The 5 Love Languages: How to Express Heartfelt Commitment to Your Mate.* Read by the author. Carol Stream, IL: Oasis Audio, 2005, Audible audio ed., 4 hr., 46 min.

Chodron, Pema. *Welcoming the Unwelcome.* Read by Claire Foy. Berkley, CA: Shambhala Publications, 2009, Audible audio ed., 4 hr., 35 min.

Chopra, Deepak. *The Book of Secrets.* Read by Daniel Passer. New York, NY: Random House Audio, 2004, Audible audio ed., 8 hr., 53 min.

Chopra, Deepak. *The Soul of Leadership: Unlocking Your Potential for Greatness.* Read by the author. New York, NY: Random House Audio, 2010. Audible audio ed., 6 hr., 6 min.

Chopra, Deepak. *The Spontaneous Fulfillment of Desire, Harnessing the Infinite Power of Coincidence.* New York, NY: Three Rivers Press, 2003.

Cloud, Henry, and John Townsend. *Boundaries in Marriage.* Grand Rapids, MI: Zondervan, 1999.

Coelho, Paulo. *The Alchemist.* Read by Jeremy Irons. New York: Harper Audio, 2004, Audible audio ed., 4 hr.

Covey, Stephen R. *Living the 7 Habits: The Courage to Change.* Read by. City: Franklin Covey on Brilliance Audio, 2005.

Covey, Stephen R. *The Eighth Habit: From Effectiveness to Greatness.* Read by the author. New York, NY: Simon & Schuster Audio, 2004. Audible audio ed., 14 hr. 23 min.

Da Outra Margem, Vislumbres. "Why to Believe in Others – Viktor Frankl." YouTube. September 11, 2015. Video, 4:21. https://www.youtube.com/watch?v=sd-1CjhbYPQ.

Daystar Television Sunday. *Power for Living with Bishop Dale C. Bronner.* Episode #SA080518, "Mouth Peace." Aired December 2, 2018. Daystar Television.

Delano, Ellie. " 'Capstone' Marriage vs 'Cornerstone Marriage.' " *Woman's Day,* May 30, 2013. https://www.womansday.com/relationships/dating-marriage/a46635/capstone-vs-cornerstone-marriage/.

DoctorRamani. "What's Gaslighting? (Individual, tribe, and societal gaslighting) – Dr. Ramani Durvasula." YouTube. April 22, 2019. Video, 11:42. https://www.youtube.com/watch?v=UTS5XsZe9Jg.

Wayne Dyer, *The Power of Intention: Learning to Co-create Your World Your Way,* Gift, Reissue edition, Carlsbad, CA: Hay House Inc., October 1, 2010, Kindle ed.

EliteBITLLIONAIRE'S M. "Become an Eagle and stop Surrounding yourself with Chickens." YouTube. November 22, 2017. Video, 5:43. https://www.youtube.com/watch?v=fQ4Rswqp_C8.

Emerson, Ralph Waldo. *Essays, First Series, Book IV.* Originally published 1841. Project Gutenberg, 2021, https://www.gutenberg.org/files/2944/2944-h/2944-h.htm.

Evans, Tony. "God Wants to Reveal Himself Through this Crisis." YouTube. May 18, 2020. video, 1:46. https://www.youtube.com/watch?v=fiKv_ZNTlPo.

Evans, Tony. Podcast, Tony Evans, *Kingdom Single* – The Urban Alternative – Listen to The Alternative with Dr. Tony Evans, Sep 18, 2018 (oneplace.com).

Fisher, Helen. *Anatomy of Love: A Natural History of Mating, Marriage, and Why We Stray.* New York, NY: W.W. Norton, 2016.

Francesco, Vissani. "Viereck's Interview to Einstein (1929)." Originally published as "What Life Means to Einstein: An Interview by George Sylvester Vierecks," in *The Saturday Evening Post*, October 26, 1929. Accessed March 1, 2020, from https://www.linkedin.com/pulse/vierecks-interview-einstein-1929-francesco-vissani-phd/.

Frankl, Viktor. *Man's Search for Meaning*. Boston: Beacon Press, 2006.

Franklin, Terry and Barbi. "You Can Tell a Lot About a Man." Released 2006. Tylis Music Group, compact disc.

Gandhi, Arun. Foreword to *Mahatma Gandhi: His Life and Ideas* by Charles F. Andrews. Woodstock, VT: Skylight Paths, 2007.

Gandhi, Mahatma.

Gaither Music TV. "Wintley Phipps – It Is Well With My Soul [Live]." YouTube. April 6, 2012. Video, 6:37. https://www.youtube.com/watch?v=E8HffdyLd0c.

Giving Voice to the Wisdom of the Ages. "I AM Discourse St Germain. 1–33 Complete." YouTube. October 19, 2019. Video, 7:45:32. https://www.youtube.com/watch?v=z5G0E2Qm6g4.

Goddard, Neville. *The Power of Awareness*. New York, NY: Penguin Random House/TarcherPerigree, 2012).

Gospel Portal. "Bishop Dale C Bronner Release Your Decree." YouTube. March 23, 2013. Video, 45:09. https://www.youtube.com/watch?v=kWooYY4rpBk.

Grenville-Cleave, Bridget. *Positive Psychology: A Practical Guide*. New York, NY: MJF Books, 2012.

Hanh, Thich Nhat. https://www.oprah.com/spirit/oprah-talks-to-thich-nhat-hanh/all#ixzz6uup9QJap.

Hagee Ministries. "The Portrait of the Mother." YouTube. May 9, 2021. Video, 28:45. (Originally aired as a TBN broadcast.)

Hanh, Thich Nhat. *Anger: Wisdom for Cooling the Flames*. New York, NY: Riverhead Books, 2002.

Hill, Napoleon. *The Law of Success: The Master Wealth-Builder's Complete and Original Lesson Plan for Achieving Your Dreams*. Originally published 1928. New York, NY: Penguin Publishing Group, 2008.

Hill, Napoleon. *Think and Grow Rich: The Landmark Bestseller—Now Revised and Updated for the 21st Century*. Revised and expanded by Dr. Arthur R. Pell. New York, NY: Penguin, 2005.

His Holiness the 14th Dalai Lama of Tibet. "Non-Violence, the Appropriate and Effective Response to Human Conflicts." Accessed February 28, 2021. https://www.dalailama.com/messages/world-peace/9-11.

Hurst, Katherine. *The Secret Law of Attraction: Master the Power of Intention*. London: Greater Minds, 2016. "Infidelity." American Association for Marriage and Family Therapy. Last updated July 2016. https://www.aamft.org/Consumer_Updates/Infidelity.aspx.

James, William. *Pragmatism and Other Writings*. New York, NY: Penguin Classics, 2000.

James, William. *The Gospel of Relaxation*.

Kehoe, John. "Changing Beliefs." n.d. John Kehoe Mind Power. https://www.learnmindpower.com/article/changing-beliefs/.

Kehoe, John. *Mind Power into the 21ˢᵗ Century*. Vancouver, Canada: Zoetic, Inc., 1996.

John Kehoe, *Secrets of the Subconscious Mind: The Easy Way to Create Success* (Secrets_of_the_Subconscious_Mind.pdf (mcusercontent.com) downloaded April 22, 2021), 2021), eBook ed.

Keller, Helen. *The Story of My Life*. Edited by John Albert Macy. New York, NY: DoubleDay, Page & Company, 1905. https://digital.library.upenn.edu/women/keller/life/life.html.

Kiyosaki, Roberts. *Rich Dad Poor Dad*. Scottsdale: Plata Publishing, 2017.

Klein, Marty. *After the Affair … What?* Sexual Intelligence, Issue 164, October 2013, http://www.sexualintelligence.org/newsletters/issue164.html.

Kohe, Martin J. *Your Greatest Power*. Read by Christopher Lane. Location: Publisher, 2014, Audible audio ed., 1 hr., 37 min.

Krippendorff, Kaihan. "Universal Law: Repeat What You Want and You Will Get It." Kaihan Krippendorff (blog). January 23, 2017. https://kaihan.net/universal-law-repeat-want-will-get/.

LaBelle, Patti. *Don't Block the Blessings*. New York, NY: Riverhead, 1996.

Marley, Bob. "Positive Vibration." Recorded 1975–1976. Tuff Gong, compact disc.

Marley, Bob. "Redemption Song." Recorded January–April 1980. Tuff Gong, compact disc.

Marley, Bob. "Trenchtown Rock." Recorded 1971. TuffGong, compact disc.

Marley, Bob, and The Wailers. "Three Little Birds." Recorded 1977. TuffGong, compact disc.

Marston, Ralph S. "Perspectives of Others." The Daily Motivator. August 6, 2015. https://greatday.com/motivate/150806.html.

Maslow, Abraham: *Maslow's Hierarchy Abraham Maslow, Maslow's Hierarchy of Needs* Explained – By Elizabeth Hopper, Updated February 24, 2020 part #7 *Love and Belonging*, Maslow's Hierarchy of Needs Explained (thoughtco.com).

May, Rollo. "Freedom and Responsibility Examined." *Behavioral Science and Guidance: Proposals and Perspectives*. Esther Lloyd-Jones and Esther M. Westervelt, eds. New York, NY: Bureau of Publications, Teachers College, Columbia University, 1963.

McGraw, Phillip C. *Life Strategies: Doing What Works, Doing What Matters*. New York, NY: Hyperion, 1999.

McHugh, Shannon V. "Are You Faking Happiness?" eCounseling. April 7, 2019. https://www.e-counseling.com/depression/ are-you-faking-happiness/.

McKay, Brett and Kate. "The Churchill School of Adulthood: A Prerequisite Class on Becoming the Author of Your Own Life." The Art of Manliness. December 11, 2020. https://www.artofmanliness.com/ articles/the-churchill-school-of-adulthood-a-prerequisite-class-on- becoming-the-author-of-your-own-life/.

McKay, Brett and Kate. "The Churchill School of Adulthood Conclusion: Thought + Action = An Awesome Adulthood." The Art of Manliness. June 6, 2021. https://www.artofmanliness.com/articles/ churchill-conclusion/.

McKay, Brett and Kate. "The Churchill School of Adulthood – Lesson #3: Live Romantically." Last modified June 3, 2021. https://www. artofmanliness.com/articles/the-churchill-school-of-adulthood- lesson-3-live-romantically/.

Miller, Andrea. "Be Beautiful, Be Yourself." [an interview with Thich Nhat Hanh], *Shambhala Sun*. November 29, 2011. https://plumvillage. org/about/thich-nhat-hanh/interviews-with-thich-nhat-hanh/ shambhala-sun-january-2012/.

Munroe, Myles. *Becoming a Leader: How to Develop and Release Your Unique Gifts*. New Kensington, PA: Whitaker House, 2018.

Munroe, Myles. *The Purpose and Power of Love & Marriage*. Shippensburg, PA: Destiny Image, 2005.

Murphy, Joseph. *The Power of Your Subconscious Mind*. New York, NY: Prentice Hall, 1994.

Nightingale, Earl. *Lead the Field*. Read by the author. Wheeling, IL: Nightingale-Conant, 2018, Audible audio ed., 2 hr., 44 min.

Nightingale, Earl. *The Strangest Secret*. Read by the author and Vic Conant. Wheeling, IL: Nightingale-Conant, 2014, Audible audio ed., 1 hr., 46 min.

Ofkirr, Vekmehel. "Bruce Lipton The Biology of Belief Full Lecture." YouTube. December 21, 2014. Video, 2:31. https://www.youtube.com/watch?v=82ShSNuru6c.

"Oh, Be Careful, Little Eyes, what you see." Hymnal.net. https://www.hymnal.net/en/hymn/c/157.

Osteen, Joel. *Your Best Life Begins Each Morning: Devotions to Start Every Day of the Year*. New York, NY: FaithWords, 2008.

Overman, Michele. "How to Identify and Deal with Passive-Aggressive People." eCounseling June 1, 2019. Accessed March 1, 2021, https://www.e-counseling.com/relationships/how-to-identify-and-deal-with-passive-aggressive-people/.

Perel, Esther. *The State of Affairs: Rethinking Infidelity*. London: Yellow Kite, 2018.

Plato. *Apology*. Translated by Benjamin Jowett. Internet Classics Archive, 2000. http://classics.mit.edu/Plato/apology.html.

Proctor, Bob. *You Were Born Rich*. Read by the author. Old Saybrook, CT: Gildan Media, 2015, Audible audio ed., 10 hr., 48 min.

Robbins, Mel. "Transform Your Life, Work and Confidence with Everyday Courage." Bay Path Women's Leadership Conference, March 28, 2019.

Rockwood, Kate. "What Happens to Your Brain When You Learn Something New." *O, The Oprah Magazine*, September 2016.

Roosevelt, Eleanor. The Faith of a First Lady: Eleanor Roosevelt's Spirituality – Truman Library Institute – Dr. Harold Ivan Smith – https://www.trumanlibraryinstitute.org/library-events/.

Ruiz, Don Miguel. *The Mastery of Love: A Practical Guide to the Art of Relationship* (A Toltec Wisdom Book). San Rafael, CA: Amber-Allen publishing, 1999.

Ruiz, Don Miguel. *The Voice of Knowledge: A Practical Guide to Inner Peace* (A Toltec Wisdom Book). San Rafael, CA: Amber-Allen publishing, 2004.

Servant, Mathieu, Peter Casey, and Geoffrey F. Woodman. "Neural Bases of Automaticity." *Journal of Experimental Psychology: Learning, Memory, and Cognition* 44, no. 3 (2018): 440–464. https://doi.org/10.1037/xlm0000454.

Shinn, Florence Scovel. *The Power of the Spoken Word*. Mansfield Centre, CT: Martino Publishing, 2016.

Skittle, Lynn. "This Is Water – Full version-David Foster Wallace Commencement Speech." YouTube. May 19, 2013 Video, 22:43. https://www.youtube.com/watch?v=8CrOL-ydFMI.

Smith, Tracy. "Emotionally Unavailable Partners and How to Spot Them." June 2, 2019. https://www.e-counseling.com/relationships/emotionally-unavailable-partners-and-how-to-spot-them/.

Stanford News. " 'You've got to find what you love,' Jobs Says." June 12, 2005. https://news.stanford.edu/2005/06/14/jobs-061505/.

Stanley, Charles. (Televised sermon).

SuperSoul Conversations Podcast by Oprah. "Oprah's SuperSoul Conversations Podcast – Pastor A. R. Bernard: Four Things Women Want from a Man." YouTube. September 11, 2017. Video, 38:23. https://www.youtube.com/watch?v=gL4ru4qXnhE.

Super Soul Sunday. "Oprah & Author Richard Rohr: The Search For our True Self." OWN, season 10, episode 1. Aired February 8, 2015.

Super Soul Sunday. "Oprah and Dr. Gary Chapman: The Five Love Languages." Omny FM. November 20, 2019. Video, 21:38. https://omny.fm/shows/oprah-s-supersoul-conversations/oprah-and-dr-gary-chapman-the-five-love-languages.

Tartt, Alduan. "True Talk: Dr Alduan Tartt and Bishop Dale Bronner (How to Have Better Relationships." YouTube. September 2, 2017. Video, 1:13:02. https://www.youtube.com/watch?v=nHDJe4GKeRI.

Taylor, Jill Bolte. *My Stroke of Insight.* New York, NY: Viking, 2006.

The Coconut Code. "The Strangest Secret in the World by Earl Nightingale full 1950." YouTube. January 1, 2015. Video, 14:24. https://www.youtube.com/watch?v=UygnXqoKrC4.

The Dalai Lama. *His Essential Wisdom.* Edited by Carol Kelly-Gangi. New York, NY: Fall River Press, 2007.

The Dalai Lama. "Message from the H.H. The Dalai Lama." *Snow Lion* 16, no. 4 (2002): page range. https://www.shambhala.com/wp/wp-content/uploads/2017/03/60.pdf.

The Entheos Initiative. "The Strangest Secret Earl Nightingale 1956 Original FULL." YouTube. January 2, 2017. Video, 31:36. https://www.youtube.com/watch?v=PeW_DMV_3Wg.

"The Music Instinct: Science and Song." Directed by Elena Mannes. Alexandria, VA: PBS, 2009. DVD.

Timeless Classic Books, "MEDITATIONS MARCUS AURELIUS ANTONINUS – Full Audio Book – Stoicism – Stoic Philosophy," YouTube. March 10, 2018. Video, 6:36:00. https://www.youtube.com/watch?v=2aoISjbpuwU.

Tolle, Eckhart. *The Power of Now: A Guide to Spiritual Enlightenment.* Read by the author Novato, CA: New World Library, 2000. Audible audio ed., 7 hr., 37 min.

Wakeman, Cy. Bay Path University's 24th Annual Women's Leadership Conference in Springfield, Massachusetts. March 2019.

Winfrey, Oprah. *What I Know for Sure.* New York, NY: Flatiron Books, 2014.

Winfrey, Oprah. *Words That Matter: A Little Book of Life Lessons.* New York, NY: HarperCollins, 2010.

Woffamily. "Look at the Birds, Bishop Dale C. Bronner, Word of Faith Family Worship Cathedral." YouTube. March 19, 2020. Video, 56:00. https://www.youtube.com/watch?v=su0mo-wp81Q.

Woffammily. "Resurrection 2012 6 am." YouTube. April 9, 2012. Video, 41:40. https://www.youtube.com/watch?v=OxFtNwBSiQ8.

Wonder, Stevie. "Mama was my greatest teacher, a teacher of compassion, love, and fearlessness. If love is sweet as a flower, then my mother is that sweet flower of love."

YouAreCreators [John Kehoe]. "All Thought Is Creative … The Powers of the Mind! (Law of Attraction)." YouTube. May 28, 2015. Video, 56:12. https://www.youtube.com/watch?v=HqD8RtyUU00.

Ziglar, Zig. Quote: *"You can have everything in life you want, if you will just help enough other people get what they want"* Ziglar Inc – Personal Development Training, Sales Coaching – Plano, Texas.

ACKNOWLEDGMENTS

To all my sincere friends and family who have been a part of my life journey and quest toward the *marrsing* mission!

To everyone who has been a special part of my life and has shared this journey with me through their love, affection, support, motivation, and appreciation of who I am as a woman, friend, wife, mother, godmother, daughter, sister, and aunty.

I thank God for the gift of life and the everyday miracles that manifest throughout each moment. I am grateful for the blessings of flow and being able to live, love, and share the grace and energy of God and the universe. I continue to be grateful for all that I have, and I will keep trusting God for all that I need.

I appreciate the wisdom and knowledge of the researchers, pastors, iconoclasts, leaders, and philosophers whose works have fueled the creation of the *marrsing* concept. I am grateful for the hard work these experts and professionals shared so that I might incorporate their knowledge into this book. They have been generous enough to extend their time and energy to benefit others by sharing their gifts with the universe. I honor the fruits of their creativity and knowledge. Their works have expanded my knowledge base and skill set while writing this invaluable book.

I hope this book will manifest from a seed of thought into a tree of transformational power.

ABOUT THE AUTHOR

Angella Watkis Francis: Founder and Chief Executive Officer—CEO of Marrsing Communications, the relationship and lifestyle company with a mission to support positive relationship transformation by helping individuals 'Turn challenges into Opportunities'.

She hails from the beautiful 'One Love' Island of Jamaica. As a native from the parish of St. Thomas, she attended Lyssons All-Age and Morant Bay High School: "'Carpe Diem' fellow MBHS." She migrated to Connecticut as a military spouse where she started her matriarchal lineage and pursued her educational advancement. She feels blessed to be a mother and enjoys spending time with family and friends.

She has pursued both private and public sector careers that have given her an eclectic array of professional experiences. She is now blazing forward on her journey of purpose and passion as an Author, Creator, Entrepreneur, and transformational Coach.

She is passionate about 'true matters of the heart and soul' and believes life is too precious to live it negatively. As an author she is fulfilling her aspiration to positively impact the world by sharing her knowledge, experiences, and wisdom to create meaningful change on a global scale. Angella is excited about her Author's journey and wants to invite others to find the opportunity to learn, grow, and thrive from every challenge that they experience.

Social Media Links

Instagram: https://www.instagram.com/marrsing_angella_w_francis

Facebook: The Power of Marrsing -Lifestyle, Relationships, Marriages &
Communications | Facebook

Facebook: Angella Francis | Facebook

LinkedIn: Angella Francis

Website: www.marrsinglife.com

I invite you to explore our website www.marrsinglife.com to connect and engage more on this innovative relationship concept. You'll find motivational materials, reading resources, and a *DIG* quiz for you to begin uncovering your greatness. You can also share your insights and opinions by joining the *Marrsing Conversations* group on Facebook.com.

I am passionate about positive relationships and how they enrich our lives with a wealth of value in well-being and happiness.

Invite Angella to Speak

Infuse enthusiasm into your next event with Angella Watkis Francis as your speaker.

Angella brings vibrancy as she inspires and motivates. She has extraordinary and eclectic entrepreneurial, relationship, and business wisdom and experiences to leverage challenges into opportunities.

Angella is passionate about sharing and motivating for positive change in the world. She wants to continue ushering you towards your greater *self.*

To inquire about Angella's availability please email her team at AWF Speaks@marrsinglife.com

Book Club Questions

To make it easier for your book club to discuss *The Power of Marrsing*, we recommend using these questions:

1. *What was your reaction to this new concept of Marrsing? How did it make you feel when you were reading it?*
2. *What is your impression of the author's audacity to create a new word and concept to frame her passion around positive relationships?*
3. *What were some of your takeaways that you can use for yourself to infuse positivity into your relationship?*
4. *The chapters can be read in any order; which chapter most resonated with you?*
5. *Was there a quote, scripture, or reference that you will use in your life and relationship?*
6. *What is your impression of the marrsing tools: Marrsing Breath, Marrsing Pause, Marrsing Clause, Marrsing DIG, Marrsing Affirmations? How can you incorporate these tools into your positive relationship transformation?*
7. *The author's marital journey could have been written from so many other perspectives, instead she chose to find the positive nuggets and create a concept that can add value to individuals, relationships, and the universe. Were you expecting more documentation of personal scenarios? Were there any particular themes in the book that a more detailed personal experience would have helped?*
8. *The author's theme from the book is about enhancing and transforming your individual self because that's where your power to effect change in your relationship comes from. What will you do first to start your transformation journey?*

CPSIA information can be obtained
at www.ICGtesting.com
Printed in the USA
BVHW092340021221
623089BV00024B/879